# Outdoor play

**JANICE FILER**

**Published by Scholastic Ltd,**
Villiers House,
Clarendon Avenue,
Leamington Spa,
Warwickshire CV32 5PR
Text © Janice Filer
© 1998 Scholastic Ltd
1 2 3 4 5 6 7 8 9 0    8 9 0 1 2 3 4 5 6 7

**Author**
Janice Filer

**Editor**
Jane Bishop

**Assistant Editor**
Lesley Sudlow

**Series designer**
Lynne Joesbury

**Designer**
Anna Oliwa

**Illustrations**
Andy Cooke

**Cover photograph**
Fiona Pragoff

Designed using Adobe Pagemaker

British Library Cataloguing-in-Publication Data
A catalogue record for this book is available from the British Library.

ISBN 0-590-53722-9

# CONTENTS

## CHAPTER 4: KNOWLEDGE AND UNDERSTANDING OF THE WORLD

## CHAPTER 5: PHYSICAL DEVELOPMENT

## CHAPTER 6: CREATIVE DEVELOPMENT

## PHOTOCOPIABLES

# INTRODUCTION

## The great outdoors

Playing outdoors is a fundamental aspect of every child's learning experience. There is immense value in playing under an ever-changing sky, in the fresh air where there is natural light and different weather conditions. The outdoors offers specific opportunities for children to satisfy their sense of adventure.

Having a safe outdoor play space in which children can run around freely, and play with a range of equipment, is an essential part of early years provision. Young children can practise their physical skills as they learn about the world around them and their place within it.

It is important to provide a stimulating outdoor environment where children can initiate, construct, pretend and create freely. At first, most outdoor play will be physical but with time it will develop to become more imaginative, realistic and progressive.

## Learning through play

Getting outdoors gives children the opportunity to take part in activities that extend their knowledge, understanding and skills and which will lay the foundations for future learning through a combination of free and structured play. Children can experience the wonderment and excitement of the outdoor environment while establishing a healthy attitude towards an active outdoor lifestyle.

Alongside the structured outdoor play activities suggested in this book, children also need free play where their learning can be extended by providing a well-structured programme which utilises a wide range of resources.

This book is designed to meet the Desirable Outcomes for Children's Learning, recommended by SCAA. *Outdoor Play* will present ideas for structured play activities in each of the identified learning areas, giving children the opportunity to meet challenges in a variety of ways in the outdoor setting.

## Setting up

The outdoor play space should provide an attractive environment which is not too daunting, nor too lacking in challenge. It needs to look attractive if it is going to stimulate the children into taking part.

The children need to be able to run around freely, use wheeled toys and small games equipment such as balls and beanbags. If possible there should also be some safe way in which children can climb, swing, hang and balance. A grassy area will provide many opportunities for outdoor play where children can exert themselves as they run up and down and push, pull and carry portable loads. An undulating surface, preferably a grassy one with some natural features such as bushes, will provide children with exciting challenges.

Whatever the size, shape or surface of the outdoor play space, it can be made attractive and inviting by the way it is set up for the children to play. Any unsightly areas can be disguised, bare walls can be brightened up and stimulating markings can be drawn on the ground, even if they are only temporary chalk marks. With a little imagination and planning, even a small concrete yard can be set up to encourage good quality outdoor play.

All children need to know how to carry outdoor equipment and how to set it up safely to suit their own needs. As the children become more competent outdoors, wheeled toys can be extended to become part of imaginative play. Fixed climbing frames can be used for more than just climbing if you provide a variety of props to transform them into imaginative play bases such as dens, boats or rockets.

Patches of garden can be designated for digging. Provide children with a range of items such as buckets, spades, old flower pots, sieves, moulds and wooden planks to use outdoors. Access to water for dampening things down and for washing dirty hands and equipment provides many opportunities for extending outdoor play. Encourage investigative play by fixing up pulleys, water trays and planks of wood to make gradients.

Outdoor resources need to be set up with care to avoid dangerous situations. Children need to help clear away messy activities so that they learn how to clear up after themselves. Keep a set of child-sized dustpans and brushes close to hand for this purpose.

## Planning and preparation

Although outdoor activities need to be planned well in advance, you will need to be flexible as well as adverse weather can preclude outdoor activity!

Prepare and collect together all your resources beforehand and decide how you are going to introduce the activities to the children, what you will say to them, what questions they might ask and what the children will do if they finish the activity more quickly than was anticipated.

## Using adult helpers

Once the children are involved in any outdoor activity, ensure that you show an interest in what they are doing, watching and giving sensitive assurance and encouragement to extend their play.

You may also need to intervene to prevent any dangerous situations from happening; explain to the children concerned why it was necessary for you to intervene. At times you will also compliment children or show delight in their accomplishments.

An adult's role is one of sensitive, constructive intervention, showing an awareness of what the children are doing, respect for a child's need for privacy and sensing when to extend their understanding. You must always be careful not to take over an activity to the extent that a child loses interest.

Many outdoor activities require you to facilitate children's learning, whilst interacting with them in a physical way. You may be a passive observer, an interested listener, a leader of the activity or game, or you may need to help children move on from a plateau by using open-ended questions to make them think.

## Resources and storage

The main resource is the outdoor play space itself and it will need to be swept or washed down regularly. It needs to be well maintained and checked regularly to remove any dangerous hazards.

All other outdoor props need to be collected together from a variety of sources. Reclaimed materials should be cleaned and made safe as young children are apt to put things into their mouths. Change the resources regularly to provide new experiences and challenges. If possible, keep a set of resources which are used just outdoors, duplicating things which the children use indoors so that they will not be disappointed when they want to play with specific items.

Each day make a note of the number of resources put out and count them back in at the end of the day. Collect them together, wash them, check them for safety and store them separately from the indoor resources in labelled containers, near the outdoor play space.

## Organisation

Ideally, your inside area should open directly onto the outdoor space so that children can have free access to it. In this case you will need to provide constant supervision outdoors as well as in. If this is not possible, plan a time when you can take the whole group of children outdoors together or take small groups outside with an adult throughout the session.

Outdoors, the children may be playing freely or they may be taking part in more structured activities. Group sizes will also vary according to the activity.

Take care not to overcrowd the outdoor area with too many children or too many resources. Children need room to run around and use their bodies in a more energetic way than they do indoors. Many outdoor activities invite bold body movements or involve the use of large-scale equipment.

Remind children of all safety issues, ground rules and boundaries each time they go outdoors, as it can become very easy for them to forget once they become involved in their play.

## Observation and assessment

Observation skills and an understanding of child development are the key to effective learning in outdoor play. Careful observation will form the basis for future planning and will help you provide effective guidance to individual children. To make the most of observation in the outdoor setting, keep a small notebook to hand to jot things down as you see them. Include in your notes things such as context, time, date, group size, type of activity, language used by the children, evaluation and recommended follow-up activities.

Outdoor movements can be fleeting so it is difficult to observe and record them. Focus on specific areas such as a child's co-ordination or balancing skills, or whether a child can use the equipment effectively. Restrict observations to short bursts of between two and five minutes, so that you can still give the children the time and attention they need to maintain interest and to extend their learning.

This outdoor observation should be used to inform future planning. As children progress at different rates, you may need to make more frequent observations for some children, being particularly sensitive when making observations of children with special needs.

## Links with home

If the children have access to an outdoor play space at home, many of the activities can be repeated or adapted without the need for any specialist equipment. Children who have no access to outdoor play space can still experience outdoor activities, even if it is only for a walk to the shops or to an outdoor play space such as the local park.

Help parents to understand the importance of getting their children outdoors on a daily basis. Talk to them, send home newsletters, photographs or examples of activities to give them ideas and to help them understand what learning experiences the children are having outdoors. Explain that children need the freedom to explore, meet challenges and take reasonable risks outdoors, and that even the smallest outdoor space can provide a wealth of opportunities for children to play.

Build upon children's own outdoor experiences to maintain a link with home. Make use of the local outdoor area for visits and walks, helping children to recognise features and make their own links with home. Invite parents in for picnics, to take part in outdoor activities, to play games, to help with outdoor maintenance or to watch outdoor performances so that they can see for themselves the value of using the outdoors.

## Health and safety

Working outdoors with children has many implications for health and safety of which you need to be fully aware. Above all your outdoor environment needs to be secure so that the children cannot get out and strangers cannot get in.

Whatever you are doing outdoors be wary of the potential hazards for young children and consider all potential danger spots. As children will be running around outside, care must be taken to prevent them from bumping into each other or equipment. Establish a set of basic outdoor ground rules which are always constant, as children need to know the outdoor boundaries and what they can or cannot do. The amount and quality of supervision should be at least the same level as for indoors.

Children need suitable outdoor clothing depending on the weather conditions and which allow freedom of movement. Parents should be encouraged to provide appropriate wear. They will need shoes with sturdy grip which can be securely fastened, clothes with no loose parts to get caught on equipment, warm coats in the winter and in the summer sunhats and/or protective clothing. At times it will of course be too hot, too cold, too wet or too slippery for children to play outdoors.

In spite of all your careful planning, accidents may still happen and appropriate first aid procedures should be in place. Concern for children's safety should be paramount at all times and it is sometimes a difficult balance to minimise the risk to them while maintaining the thrill of challenge. Only by 'doing' will young children learn to assess risk for themselves and learn to be safe.

Fixed play equipment should comply with current recognised standards, such as the British Standard 5696 and all outdoor equipment needs regular cleaning and maintenance.

Throughout this book there are reminders of safety issues, highlighted by the CARE! warning to alert you to any potential dangers.

## How to use this book

The chapters in this book are organised according to the six Areas of Learning for the under-fives that have been identified by the School Curriculum and Assessment Authority. These areas are Language and Literacy (Chapter 1), Mathematics (Chapter 2), Personal and Social Development (Chapter 3), Knowledge and Understanding of the World (Chapter 4), Physical Development (Chapter 5) and Creative Development (Chapter 6). All the outdoor play activities described in this book are directly linked to these areas of learning.

The activities are practical ideas which are designed to take place in a variety of outdoor play settings, although many of them can be adapted for use in other areas including indoor space. Each activity is based around a key learning objective and the ideas are planned to stimulate and develop young children's outdoor play experiences in a safe enjoyable way.

For each activity, advice is given about the ideal group size, what resources are needed, how to set up the activity and how to carry it out with the children. A selection of questions to ask relating to the activity are suggested. In addition, there are ideas to help you adapt the main activity to meet the needs of older and younger children. Follow-up ideas are also given linking with other areas of the curriculum.

At the end of the book there is a section with six photocopiable sheets which are cross-referenced and related to a specific activity detailed earlier in the book. There is also a photocopiable 'topic web' on page 10 which shows all the outdoor activities in the book with their page references.

# OUTDOOR PLAY

*The outdoor activities in this chapter provide ways to encourage the development of children's language and literacy skills. Some of the activities extend talking and listening skills while others support stories, rhymes and role-play.*

# SCAVENGER'S LETTER LINKS

**Learning objective**
*To look for objects outside with the same letter as the children's initials.*

**Group size**
*Up to six children.*

## What you need
A piece of paper for each child, some marker pens, a notepad, large sheet of sugar paper or a whiteboard.

## Setting up
Write the initial letter of each child's name on separate sheets of paper.

## What to do
Give each child the piece of paper with their own initial written on it. Discuss the initials and their letter sounds and tell the children how other objects may start with the same letter. Give them plenty of examples to help them grasp the concept and to be fully aware of their own 'sound'.

Take the children on a hunt around the garden to discover what objects they can find starting with the same letter as their own initials. Write the words down in a notebook for each child while you are outside, emphasising that the first letters are all the same. Compare the sounds as well as the shapes of the letters.

Back indoors, write up the list for each child under their name either on a large sheet of sugar paper or a whiteboard. Count the lists of words to find out whose name has the longest list of objects, and to find out which letter is the most popular one. Encourage an awareness of letter links by asking the children to look for similar letters in the writing they see around them.

## Questions to ask
What is the first letter of your name? Do you know anything else which starts with the same letter? Can you write the first letter of your name? Have you seen the letter anywhere else?

## For younger children
Write each child's name and point out any similarities between their initials and the lists of the objects you have recorded for them.

## For older children
Encourage the older children to make a list of the first letter of their names several times on a sheet of paper. They can add the rest of the word when they find an object starting with the same letter.

**Follow-up activities**
• Look for initial letters in written signs.
• Print notices to display outdoors and see if the children can find and count how many times their initial letters appear.
• Look for the children's initials in print when you are looking at books together.

# SCRIBING IN THE SAND

**Learning objective**
*To convey meaning through drawing pictures in sand.*

**Group size**
*Pairs.*

## What you need
Two large shallow trays, silver sand, a jug of water.

## Setting up
Cover the surface of both trays with a fine layer of sand. Place the trays outside on an even surface.

## What to do
Tell the children that they are going to make marks in the sand using their fingers. Explain that they can each draw something and then their partner can guess what they have drawn. Challenge the children to experiment with drawing and writing using their fingers in different ways.

Encourage them to make marks in the sand by using their index fingers as pencils, using two fingers together, making thumb prints or using a fist to make larger marks. The children could pretend to make secret messages and codes for each other to decipher. Help the children to understand that words and pictures can convey meaning to others by pretending to write simple messages in the sand yourself.

After a while, pour a little water in one of the trays to dampen the sand. The children will then be able to make deeper impressions in the damp sand. Repeat the activity using wet sand. Discuss the difference between drawing in wet sand and drawing in dry sand.

Ask the children to search around the outdoor play area for objects to use for scribing in the sand. Encourage them to experiment with feathers, small twigs, stones or lolly sticks.

## Questions to ask
Can you make a mark in the sand? What does the sand feel like? Can you make lines, squiggles or fingerprints in the sand? Can you copy what I have drawn in the sand? Can you guess what your friend has drawn in     the sand? What things can you find around the outdoor play area to make marks in the sand? What else can you do?

## For younger children
Younger children could just make patterns and marks in the sand with their fingers, experiencing the difference between wet and dry sand.

## For older children
Older children could practise making marks in the sand to represent the letters of their names. They could practise writing their names by going over the shape you have already marked out.

**Follow-up activities**
• Take it in turns to draw with a finger on each other's back, then guess what has been drawn. After three guesses reveal the symbol!
• Repeat the main activity using a mixture of cornflour and water.
• Try using finger paints to draw.

# MARKS IN MUD

## What you need
A garden area with mud, a jug of water, a note book, pen. For each child you also need one twig, one lolly stick, one piece of card (12cm × 6cm), glue, some marker pens.

## Setting up
Check your chosen area for safety, making sure there are no dangerous objects lying around and that the children will be enclosed. Decide upon a short, winding route within the outdoor space and find or create patches of mud for the children to make their messages. Use some water to dampen down the earth patches to facilitate the task.

## What to do
Ask the children to each make a marker flag by drawing a bold design on a piece of card and gluing it onto a lolly stick. Explain that the markers will indicate the areas in the garden where they are going to make a trail and leave messages for the other group to follow. Tell the children the purpose of the trail saying that it could lead to a place of interest, to lost treasure or to a picnic spot.

Give each child a twig and tell the children to make marks in the damp soil for their message. The adult leading the group needs to carry a note book and pen to record the message for future use. Complete the trail by writing a message and pushing a marker flag into the ground at regular intervals along the route.

Invite the other group to follow the trail by searching for the markers and reading the messages left in the mud. Repeat the activity to give all children the experience of setting and following a trail.

### Questions to ask
What does your message say? How will the people following the trail know what your message means? Do you know of any other ways people leave messages for each other? Have you noticed any signs around you? What do the signs mean?

## For younger children
Younger children could use their fingers to make marks in the mud. They could hide the marker flags to play a hunting game.

## For older children
Older children could plan their own activity, they could clear their own patches of earth and then use a variety of scribing tools such as feathers, sticks and carving tools to create different marks and symbols with specific meanings.

### Follow-up activities
• Set up trays of wet soil outdoors for children to practise writing and drawing.
• Make marks in different mediums such as Plasticine, dough or clay, using a range of mark-making tools, some conventional, some improvised.
• Draw up a map to record the activity.
• Make and follow footprints in the mud.
• Go on a sign-spotting walk around the local environment.

# WHERE'S TEDDY?

*Learning objective*
To use a story to develop positional language.

*Group size*
Up to eight children.

## What you need
A copy of *We're Going on a Bear Hunt* by Michael Rosen and Helen Oxenbury (Walker Books), a large teddy bear, two or three old blankets, some outdoor play equipment set up as an obstacle course.

## Setting up
Look at the book *We're Going on a Bear Hunt* for inspiration and set up an obstacle trail to correspond to the actions in the story (include going through a tunnel, crawling under a sheet or over a bench for example). Make a 'cave' using the blankets at the end of the course and hide the teddy bear inside.

## What to do
Read the story *We're Going on a Bear Hunt* to the children. Explain that you are all going on a bear hunt in the garden. Refer them back to the pictures in the story and demonstrate the actions. Focus on the positional language such as under, over, through and back as used in the story to describe the bear hunt. Practise these actions to make sure the children clearly understand them.

Begin the course and encourage the children to chant the appropriate positional words as they travel along it. As they reach the end, challenge them to find the hidden teddy. Once teddy has been found tell them they have to go back along the obstacle course to home (where they started!).

Afterwards ask the children to recall the sequence of events on the way to find the bear. Make a game by saying teddy is coming and show him crawling back under... walking back through... jumping back over... crawling back under... walking back through and jumping back over to further reinforce the positional language.

## Questions to ask
Can you do the actions to match the words in the story? What would you do if you met a real bear? Have you ever felt scared? What did it feel like?

## For younger children
Play going on a bear hunt in the garden. When the children meet the 'scary' teddy they must run back to a pre-determined place of safety.

## For older children
Encourage older children to set up their own bear hunt and take it in turns to hide the teddy bear at the end. Give them the blankets to make their own cave.

### Follow-up activities
• Hunt for other 'beasts' in the garden.
• Set up more complex routes to the cave. Encourage the use of positional language (over, under, through and back) to recall the activity.
• Ask the children to climb over, crawl through or under objects they find in the garden. CARE! Check out the area beforehand to remove any dangerous objects. Remind the children of any safety issues, boundaries or guidelines concerning what they can or cannot do in your outdoor play space.
• Hide a small teddy in the garden and help the children to find it by giving positional clues.

# WEATHER WATCH

## What you need
Some examples of weather charts and weather symbols, a large sheet of card, several sheets of white A4 paper, felt-tipped pens, scissors, Blu-Tack, photocopiable page 59.

## Setting up
Show the children some conventional weather charts and symbols to encourage discussion about symbols conveying meaning.

## What to do
Discuss different types of weather with the children asking them to name the different combinations of weather which we might experience. Ask a different child to suggest an appropriate description of the weather each day.

Make a chart with the days of the week at the top using the large sheet of card (see illustration or use photocopiable page 59), and give each child some card, scissors and felt-tipped pens to design their own weather symbol. Ask each child to make a different symbol. When they have done this, make several copies of each symbol and ask the children to put some Blu-Tack on the back of each one. Display the chart in a prominent position where the children can reach it.

Take the children outdoors to see what the weather is like. Talk together about the weather conditions encouraging the children to say whether it is warm or cold, if the sun is shining, the wind blowing or rain falling.

Back indoors ask one of the children to put up the correct symbols on your chart to show the weather. Use the appropriate symbol to record daily weather conditions throughout the week, with different children being asked to contribute.

## Questions to ask
What is the weather like today? What kind of weather do you like best? How do you feel on a rainy day? What do you do when it rains? What do you do when it is sunny?

## For younger children
Take younger children outside regularly to feel and see what the weather is like for themselves. Point out the different weather conditions whenever they are playing outdoors.

## For older children
Encourage older children to develop their own ways of recording the weather, making their own charts and symbols to use on a regular basis. Encourage them to listen to weather forecasts on the radio or television when they are at home.

**Follow-up activities**
• Make a display of summer and winter clothes.
• Discuss what sort of activities you might do on a dry day, a rainy day, a cold day, a windy day or a sunny day.
• Draw or paint a picture to depict the weather, explaining about warm and cold colours.
• Make a weather mobile using the symbols made for the weather chart, suspend it from a tree or a fence and watch it moving in the wind.

# LIFT SOME LITTER

*Learning objective*
*To use writing for a specific purpose.*

*Group size*
*Up to six children.*

## What you need
A plastic container and a pair of rubber or disposable gloves for each child, a large sheet of sugar paper, marker pens, scissors.

## Setting up
Prepare a litter analysis chart by dividing the sugar paper into two columns. Give each child a pair of rubber gloves and a container for litter. CARE! Ensure that an adult checks the outdoor area being used and removes any dangerous objects. Explain any ground rules, boundaries and safety issues, telling the children to check with an adult if they come across any objects they are not sure about.

## What to do
Explain to the children that you are going on a litter hunt. Give each child a container and tell them to wear the rubber gloves.

Take the children outdoors and encourage them to collect up whatever litter they can find. Supervise the children at all times to ensure they are not injured by any sharp items. Once you have a collection, gather the children together to look at the litter.

Decide upon two categories into which the litter can be sorted. These could be natural objects and manufactured ones or all the brightly coloured objects and all the dull coloured objects.

Back indoors, make a chart by writing in the two categories at the top of your piece of sugar paper. Sort the litter, making a tick on the chart underneath the relevant category. Tot up all the marks to discover what kind of litter is the most common. Discuss and compare what has been found.

## Questions to ask
How did the litter get into the outdoor play area? What can you do with all the litter you have found? What should you do with your litter? What happens to all the litter lying around?

## For younger children
Help younger children to sort the litter according to simple criteria such as small pieces and large pieces. Ask the children to make a mark on the chart for each piece of litter found. Count the marks together out loud.

## For older children
Let the children decide for themselves ways to display and record their findings. Encourage them to sort according to more than one criteria. For example, all the natural, small pieces of litter could be represented by a simple, repeated brown circle. Use more than two columns on the analysis chart.

**Follow-up activities**
• Find creative ways of displaying the litter.
• Go litter hunting in the same area regularly over a period of time. Compare and record the different types of litter found.
• Make posters to deter litter dropping and fix them to some containers placed outside to use as litter bins.

# BIRD CHARTS

*Learning objective*
*To develop vocabulary through observing, recording and talking about the birds outside.*

*Group size*
*Up to six children.*

## What you need
Clipboards (one for each child), drawing paper, marker pens, reference book of birds.

## Setting up
Make a simple tally chart for each child (see below). Ask the children to draw bird shapes at the top of the chart to represent different birds. Give each child a clipboard, drawing paper and some marker pens.

## What to do
Start by showing the children some of the birds in the reference book. Look at the individual markings on a number of birds, for example the red breast of the robin or the black and white plumage of the magpie.

Entice the birds into the outdoor play area by scattering some bird seed around the ground. As the birds arrive into the area try and name them, describing their distinctive features, noticing different sizes, colours and shapes. Look at similarities, pointing out that all birds have wings, feathers and beaks. Encourage the children to repeat and join in the naming process to help them learn new vocabulary. By hearing these new words in a meaningful context, the children will develop the confidence to use the words themselves. Throughout the session, watch and record the birds that come into the outdoor play space by making a mark under the appropriate symbols on the tally chart.

Later, count the numbers of each species recorded on the chart. Discuss and display the chart with pictures of all the birds recorded. Encourage the children to describe and recite the names of the birds they have seen. Help them understand why the birds have come into the play area.

## Questions to ask
Which birds have you seen? What do they look like? Why do you think the birds have come into the garden? How many different types of birds have you spotted? How many birds have you counted?

## For younger children
Distinguish between big birds and little birds, blackbirds and brightly coloured birds. Choose two or three common birds to look for and encourage the children to name and count the birds as they see them.

## For older children
Encourage older children to make their own charts. Show them how to use the reference book to identify some of the birds. Repeat the activity regularly and encourage the children to make observations and recordings over a longer period of time.

**Follow-up activities**
• Make play dough models of birds.
• Sing the nursery rhymes 'Four and twenty blackbirds' and 'Two little dicky birds'.
• Make a bird mobile using photocopiable page 60.
• Make some bird food by mixing melted lard, biscuit crumbs, nuts and dried fruit. Put the mixture in empty yoghurt pots, wait for it to harden and hang it from a tree. Watch the birds feeding from inside your room.

# MARKET STALLS

**Learning objective**
*To increase vocabulary and language competence through role playing.*

**Group size**
*Six to eight children.*

## What you need
A table for each stall, money containers, recycled materials to represent produce, large sheets of paper, marker pens, sturdy cardboard, scissors, play money.

## Setting up
Arrange the tables to represent a market. Make signs for all the stalls and fix them to the tables. Place a variety of goods and some play money in the containers on each table.

## What to do
If possible arrange a visit to a local market place as preparation for this activity. Encourage children to watch and listen to the way people buy and sell things to each other.

Start the activity with discussion about what markets are, reminding the children of their visit to the market. Discuss the idea of setting up a market in the outdoor play space and allow the children to decide what type of stalls they will have. These may differ according to the geographical area or the time of year. A busy city might have a market place with food, clothes and antique stalls; a country market might have animal, craft and flower stalls; a seaside market might sell fish.

Ask the children to search through their belongings for items to pretend to sell. They could make items for sale by cutting out shapes from sturdy card or using recycled materials such as empty plastic bottles, boxes and cardboard tubes. Invite the children to arrange the goods for sale on the tables as you would for a market. Give each child some plastic money.

Encourage the children to role-play the scenes of a busy market place. Challenge them to buy and sell goods to each other.

## Questions to ask
Have you ever been to a market? What was it like? What did you buy? What do you have for sale on your market stall? How much does it cost to buy?

### For younger children
Set up a stall with some of the children's toys and give the children some pretend money. Pretend to be the stallholder and encourage the children to visit the stall to buy back their toys.

### For older children
Let older children plan their own outdoor market, setting up their own stalls. Encourage them to use market banter during their role-play. Leave the stalls set up for several days to allow the play to develop.

**Follow-up activities**
• Set up different types of stalls on different days of the week. You could have a fish market, a craft market or a flower market.
• Make some real things to sell; plants they have grown, pictures they have drawn, squash and cakes they have made.
• Use real money.
• Have a multicultural market theme displaying articles from different countries.

# MATHEMATICS

## CHAPTER TWO

*Outdoor play can provide opportunities for children to take part in practical mathematical activities. The ideas in this chapter help to develop the children's knowledge of quantity, capacity, volume, shape, matching pattern, sequence, time, counting, size, sorting and grading.*

# SCOOPING CONKERS

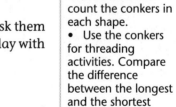

**Learning objective**
*To develop an understanding of quantity through scooping and weighing conkers.*

**Group size**
*Up to six children.*

## What you need
A deep outdoor tray, enough conkers to fill the tray, six scoops, six plastic containers (such as ice cream tubs).

## Setting up
Take the children out during the autumn to collect conkers. Talk about the conkers as you collect them, counting how many each child has found. Store them until you are ready to use them. When you are ready, position the tray outdoors filled with conkers.

## What to do
If appropriate, start by reminding the children of the time they went conker collecting. Give each child a scoop and a container and let them experiment playing with the conkers. Invite the children to scoop up the conkers in the tray, suggesting that they fill their plastic container with them. Count the number of conkers each child has scooped into the container. Return all the conkers to the tray and repeat the activity several times.

Compare and discuss the different quantities of conkers used throughout the activity and point out the number of conkers in the tray. Re-enforce mathematical language such as add more, take away a few, many, a couple, full, half-full, empty. Ask the children to compare how many conkers there are in a flat scoop with how many there are in a heaped scoopful.

### Questions to ask
Where did the conkers come from? Have you ever been conker picking? What time of the year do you look for conkers? How many conkers do you think there are in the tray? How many little conkers fit into the container? How many large conkers fit into it?

### For younger children
Position an adult to work with the children and ask them to encourage the children to count the conkers as they play with them.

### For older children
Older children could work co-operatively in pairs to estimate and compare the quantities of conkers they are using.

**Follow-up activities**
• Repeat the activity using different sized scoops and containers to increase understanding of quantity, capacity and volume.
• Draw mathematical shapes on the ground with chalk. Fill the outlines with conkers and count the conkers in each shape.
• Use the conkers for threading activities. Compare the difference between the longest and the shortest string of conkers.

# SORTING SHAPES

*Learning objective*
To recognise two-dimensional shapes occurring in patterns found outdoors.

*Group size*
Four children.

## What you need
Templates (approximately 8cm × 8cm) of the two-dimensional shapes of a square, a triangle, a circle and a rectangle, some card, a marker pen, scissors.

## Setting up
Use the templates to make a set of shapes for each child. Show the shapes to the children and ask them to name the shapes they know. Reinforce the children's knowledge of the shapes by asking them to name each shape in turn.

## What to do
Explain to the children that they are going to go outside to look for things which are the same shapes as those they have been talking about.

Give each child a set of the shapes you made in advance and challenge them to search around the outdoor area to find a shape to match it. Look for shapes in bricks, window panes, paving slabs, roof tiles or screw heads.

Ask the children to point out the shapes they find. Repeat the activity until each child has had the opportunity to find something which is a square, a triangle, a circle and a rectangle.

## Questions to ask
Can you name the shapes you found in the outdoor play space? Can you match them to the set of shapes you have with you? Can you describe the difference between a square and a rectangle? What shape did you see most often? Did you find any patterns outdoors which use the same shapes over and over again?

## For younger children
Ask an adult to accompany the children on a shape-spotting walk around the grounds. Point out and name the shapes you see and encourage the children to do the same.

## For older children
Give older children an assortment of shapes. Send them off on their own to match up the shapes with anything they can find outside. Encourage older children to make comparisons and to articulate their discoveries using mathematical language.

**Follow-up activities**
• Draw the patterns seen on brickwork or roof tiles.
• Go on an outdoor walk and search for straight lines, curves, symmetrical or asymmetrical patterns.
• Draw large circles, triangles, squares and rectangles on the ground with chalk. Hold up a shape card as a cue to the children to stand on the corresponding drawn shape. Repeat the activity several times revealing different shaped cue cards.

# 'WHAT'S THE TIME?'

*Learning objective*
*To play an action game to develop an understanding of the sequence of time.*

*Group size*
*Up to six children.*

## What you need
Some chalk, a picture of a wolf, a large, safe outdoor play space.

## Setting up
Draw a chalk line on the ground in the outdoor play space to represent the wolf's home. Draw another chalk line twenty metres from the first line.

## What to do
Show the children the picture of the wolf and explain that the wolf is hungry! Stand on the first line with your back to the children pretending to be the hungry wolf. Invite the children to stand behind the other line.

The children taunt the wolf by chanting 'What's the time Mr Wolf?' When the wolf replies 'two o'clock', the children move two steps forward. When the wolf replies 'three o'clock', they take three steps forward and so on. The wolf can turn around to try and catch the children moving towards him at any time, anyone caught moving goes back to the base line to start again. The chanting continues until the wolf calls out 'dinner time.' He then chases the children back to the line, hopefully catching one of them for his dinner! The children are out when they are touched by the wolf. The last child caught becomes the wolf. Any child who creeps up to the wolf's back before 'dinner time' also becomes 'Mr Wolf'.

## Questions to ask
Do you know any stories about a hungry wolf? What time do you get up in the morning? What time do you have your dinner? What time do you go to bed? What do you do when you feel hungry?

## For younger children
With younger children an adult could be Mr Wolf every time the game is played. Use only the commands 'one o'clock' and 'two o'clock' and 'dinner time'. Walk with the children as they take footsteps towards the wolf.

## For older children
Increase the difficulty of the game by using all the hourly times to represent a different activity in the wolf's daily life cycle. For example, eight o'clock could be bedtime, which is the cue for the children to pretend to be asleep.

**Follow-up activities**
• Count the number of footsteps it takes to reach certain destinations.
• Using a clock with moveable hands, encourage the children to recite the hourly times in a clockwise direction.
• Play 'Grandma's footsteps' where children creep up behind an adult while her back is turned. When she turns round and looks, they must stop. The child to touch her back becomes Grandma.
• Re-enact some of the story lines of traditional wolf stories such as *Little Red Riding Hood* and *The Three Little Pigs.*

# PILE OF BONES

## Learning objective
To encourage an understanding of addition and subtraction.

## Group size
Up to six children.

## What you need
The story *Funnybones* by Janet and Allan Ahlberg (Mammoth), one flowerpot (9cm/3.5in), 10 cardboard or plastic tubes (11cm), two pieces of string (130cm and 60cm long) for each child. A large cloth, some marker pens.

## Setting up
Put the flowerpots, tubes and string in a pile on the cloth outside. Make up a sample skeleton. Draw a face on the flowerpot. Make a hole on both sides of the cardboard tube representing the shoulders. Secure the longest piece of string to another tube and thread it through three tubes, into the holes made in the shoulder piece, up through the flowerpot head. Tie to make a loop. Thread the string back down through the tubes representing the shoulders and body, into two more tubes to make the other leg. Secure the string. Take the short length of string, using the remaining tubes to make the arms. Secure the string at both ends.

## What to do
Read *Funnybones* to the children before your begin the activity.

Show the children the sample skeleton. Explain about bones and name the main body parts. Tell the children the pile of tubes and flowerpots represent the bones. Let them choose one flowerpot and ten tubes to make a whole skeleton. Count the parts as you demonstrate the activity, adding or subtracting the tubes one at a time. Explain that the number of bones used to make the skeleton remains the same whether they are piled up together or spaced apart, even though they look different. Invite the children to play with their skeletons.

## Questions to ask
How many bones do you need to make the skeleton? Which looks the biggest, the pile of bones or the whole skeleton? Can you feel your own bones through your skin?

## For younger children
Make a simple model using six tubes instead of ten. Name and count the bones. Match the skeleton's bones to the corresponding parts of their own body.

## For older children
Complete the activity as a team game. Tell the children to run, one at a time, to collect a tube or flowerpot to take back to make up the whole skeleton. Decorate the model skeleton to make it look more realistic.

## Follow-up activities
• Use the skeletons as puppets to dramatise scary stories.
• Photocopy the template on page 61, cut out the bones, muddle them and ask the children to put them back together in the right order.
• Using several copies of the photocopiable sheet, make a pile of bones. Invite the children one at a time, to take the bones and build a skeleton. Remind them that they need ten sections to complete the task.

# TARGETS OF TEN

**Learning objective**
*To encourage counting up to ten.*

**Group size**
*Up to four children.*

## What you need
A large bucket, ten small beanbags, chalk.

## Setting up
Place the bucket in a space in the outdoor area. Draw a chalk circle around the bucket, approximately four metres in diameter. Hide the beanbags all around the area you are going to use to play the game.

## What to do
Challenge the children to find the beanbags and count how many each child finds. Now invite the children to stand on the outer edge of the circle to throw the beanbags into the bucket and count the number of beanbags that each child throws into the bucket. Record scores by marking a line on a piece of paper each time the child gets a beanbag into the bucket.

The child who throws the most beanbags into the bucket can take a turn to hide them all around the outdoor play space ready to restart the game. Repeat the game several times to give all children the opportunity to hide and count the beanbags.

## Questions to ask
Can you find all the beanbags? How many bean bags can you find? Can you count the number of beanbags in the bucket? Can you throw the beanbags under arm? Can you throw them over arm? Can you throw the beanbags with one hand? Can you throw the beanbags with two hands?

## For younger children
Match the number of beanbags you hide to the counting ability of the children involved. Count the beanbags with the children as they place them in the bucket.

## For older children
Increase the degree of difficulty by using a smaller bucket and making the distance bigger between the chalk line and the bucket. Give older children a set amount of time to throw all the beanbags back into the bucket.

**Follow-up activities**
• Try hiding and throwing different objects such as quoits, skittles, batons and balls.
• Decorate a piece of card with a face and cut an open mouth – throw the beanbags into the mouth!
• Hide ten different objects outside and let the children take it in turns to find and count the ten objects they find.

# FINDING FAMILIES

*Learning objective*
To grade objects found in the garden into small, medium and large.

*Group size*
Up to six children.

## What you need
Three cardboard boxes, three sheets of paper, some butterfly clips, scissors, glue, a marker pen.

## Setting up
Fix the boxes together, using the butterfly clips, to make a house or block of flats which will house the objects the children find. Cut the paper to fit inside each box. Write the headings small, medium and large separately on the three sheets of paper and glue the paper as carpets inside the boxes. There is now a room for large objects, a room for medium objects, and a room for small objects.

## What to do
Explain to the children that they are going outdoors to look for 'families' of objects. Explain that these should be objects that are the same apart from size such as a large, medium and small stone. Show the children that there is a room in the house for all the small objects, another room for all the medium-sized objects and a third room for all the large objects.

Make your collection outdoors and ensure that the children have found relevant items. Back indoors, invite the children to sort the objects they collect by putting them into the rooms in the house according to their size.

Challenge the children to find and sort at least three sets of objects. They could find three different sized stones, leaves or twigs. Compare the sizes of the objects to reinforce the idea of grading according to size.

## Questions to ask
Can you point to all the small objects? Can you show me all the medium objects? Where are all the large objects? Why are the objects different? Can you see any objects of the same family? Can you count all the small objects? Can you count all the medium objects and all the large objects?

## For younger children
Use two boxes only and grade objects into big and little. In the same way point out similarities and differences between the items to the children.

## For older children
Increase the number of objects the children need to find and sort. Encourage older children to find their own way of recording the activity, or to develop different sorting criteria (colour, shape).

**Follow-up activities**
• Read traditional stories about graded sizes, such as *Goldilocks and the Three Bears* and *The Billy Goats Gruff*.
• Display collections of 'families' such as Russian dolls.
• Take a walk around the outdoor area and look for objects to grade according to size such as flowerpots, trees, flowers or chimney pots.

# FILL THE TUBE

*Learning objective*
*To discover how many objects will fit into an empty sweet tube.*

*Group size*
*Up to six children.*

## What you need
Six small empty sweet tubes, a variety of tiny outdoor objects (seeds, stones, leaves), a sheet of writing paper, a marker pen.

## Setting up
Ask the children to bring in empty sweet tubes from home and store them until you need to use them for this activity. Fill one of the tubes with as many tiny outdoor objects as possible then spread the articles out on a piece of paper and demonstrate how they all fit into the empty sweet tube. Prepare a list of the children's names. Check the outdoor play space to make sure it is safe to play in.

## What to do
Invite the children to go outdoors and explain that they are going on a scavenger hunt to look for tiny outdoor objects to fill up their empty sweet tubes. CARE! Warn the children not to put any little objects in their mouth. Explain the concept of a scavenger hunt. Tell the children the boundaries and give them a set time of approximately fifteen minutes to look for things to put in their empty tubes.

Before the hunt begins, ask the children to make estimates about how many things they think will fit into the tubes. Record each child's estimate on a piece of paper.

When the time is up, count the objects in each child's tube to see who has collected the most. After the count, challenge the children to put the objects back into their tubes. Discuss the activity with the children, focusing on quantity and size. Compare the children's estimates with their final scores.

## Questions to ask
What was in the tube before? How many sweets do you think the tube contained? What size objects will fit into the empty sweet tube? Where did you find the small objects that fit into your tube? Can you squeeze any more objects into the tube? Can you guess how many objects there are in your tube? Can you count them?

## For younger children
Hunt for a specified number of objects within the children's counting ability. For example, challenge the children to find five small objects to put into their tube.

## For older children
Older children can work together in pairs to fill the tubes. They can count and record the number of objects they have managed to fit into the tube. Ask them to find creative ways to display the small objects or make a collage with them.

### Follow-up activities
• Go on a scavenger hunt to look for specific things; green objects, different kinds of leaves or different types of stones.
• Hide objects around the outdoor area and invite the children to search for the objects you have hidden.
• Play treasure hunts; choose ten items to be the treasure and allow children to take it in turns to hide and hunt for the treasure around the outdoor play space.
• Play a game of hide-and-seek.

# CAPTAIN'S CALLING

*Learning objective*
To play a nautical game using mathematical language.

*Group size*
Up to eight children.

## What you need
Some pictures illustrating sailors, ships and nautical scenes. Chalk, a large outdoor space.

## Setting up
Show the children the pictures of ships and sailors and tell them that they are going to play a game called 'Captain's calling'. Chalk a large boat shape on the ground to represent the deck of a ship.

## What to do
Explain that a captain (you) is in charge of a ship (the deck shape you have marked out on the ground) and gives orders to the crew (the children) who always do exactly what they are told! Invite the children to stand on the deck (inside the outline of the ship) and say that you will call out commands to keep the crew in order as the ship sails upon the sea.

On the cue, 'Captain's coming', the sailors must stand to attention, saluting the captain. You then command them to take two steps to the left and so on. Use five directional commands according to the children's knowledge and ability ('forwards', 'backwards', 'to the left', 'to the right', 'turn round in circles'). Make up actions to match the orders which you are calling out.

Before the game starts help the children to practise responding to the commands with the corresponding actions until they grasp the idea of the game. Remind them to use the whole space and not to touch each other or move outside the boundary lines of the ship.

Invite the children to move according to the instructions which you call out. Anyone who gets the actions wrong or who responds too slowly, is called out to sit on the side lines. The game is over when every child has been called out.

## Questions to ask
Can you hold up your left hand? Can you hold up your right hand? How do you walk backwards? Can you turn around on the same spot? Do you know any songs about sailors or ships? Have you ever seen a big ship? Have you ever been on a boat?

## For younger children
Reduce the number of commands to three and keep them simple.

## For older children
Increase the commands in number and difficulty, calling them out in quick succession. Encourage older children to make up their own commands and take it in turns to be the captain.

## Follow-up activities
• Repeat the game using commands and actions associated with life at sea, such as, 'person overboard', 'climb the rigging',' walk the plank', 'hoist the flag', 'scrub the decks', 'as the crow flies'.
• Use comical commands – 'jelly wobble', 'seasick sailor', 'chicken walk' or scary ones – 'storm brewing', 'shipwreck', 'shark aboard', 'pirates landed'.
• Learn songs about the sea, such as 'I like to sail in my big blue boat', 'The big ship sails', 'Row, row, row your boat', 'Bobby Shaftoe' *This Little Puffin* (Young Puffin).

# PERSONAL AND SOCIAL DEVELOPMENT

## CHAPTER THREE

*In these activities children will be encouraged to play co-operatively, to understand the difference between right and wrong, to take turns, to share, to be aware of personal hygiene, to develop independence and to respect themselves, each other and property.*

# I'VE LOST MY HAT

*Learning objective*
*To learn to look after property by playing a searching game to find a hat.*

*Group size*
*Up to eight children.*

### What you need
A safe outdoor space, a straw hat, some red ribbon.

### Setting up
Tie the red ribbon around the brim of the hat. Discuss the importance of looking after our own possessions and helping each other to find things if they become lost. Hide the hat in the outdoor play space before going outdoors with the children.

### What to do
Before going outside explain to the children that while you were out walking, the wind blew your hat off and you lost it. Explain that you cannot find your hat anywhere and that you would like them to help you find it.

Invite the children outdoors to help you to look for your hat. When the hat is found the child who finds it restarts the game by hiding it again for the other children to find.

### Questions to ask
Have you ever lost anything special? How did you feel? Did you find it? When you find something that has been lost, how do you feel?

### For younger children
Wear the hat on a walk around the outdoor play space with the younger children. Let it secretly slip off your head. When the children notice you are no longer wearing the hat, retrace your steps so that they can help you find it.

### For older children
Hide the hat so that there is no sign of the red ribbon as a clue and challenge the children to locate it.

---

**Follow-up activities**
• Hide a dressing-up hat in the grounds and send the children off to retrieve it. The child who finds it has to make up a funny dance, sketch or make a funny face.
• Set up an outdoor hat shop.
• Design and make a hat to wear outdoors.
• Make pirates' hats to wear outdoors by folding a large sheet of newspaper.

# TRAFFIC LIGHTS

**Learning objective**
*To learn how to respond to a signal.*

**Group size**
*Up to ten children.*

## What you need
A photograph of a set of traffic lights, three pieces of card, scissors, a red, amber and green marker pen, a circular object to draw around (such as a small saucer), a flat, safe outdoor play space.

## Setting up
Draw around the saucer three times on the piece of card and colour the circles red, amber and green. Cut out the circles and use them to represent the traffic lights.

## What to do
Talk about traffic lights and where we might see them. Ask the children to name the colours of a set of traffic lights and invite them to recall what happens when the lights change colour. Discuss the purpose of using signs rather than language. Talk about the ways people communicate with each other when they cannot see or hear.

Check the outdoor play space to ensure that it is safe to use for an action game. Explain the boundaries of the game to the children and discuss all safety aspects such as looking where you are going when you run, stopping or sitting down on the ground in a controlled manner.

Explain to the children that the coloured circles represent the traffic lights. Tell them that when you hold up a green circle it's a sign to run around, the red circle is a signal to stop running and stand still, and an amber signal indicates they should sit down. If the red circle is held up after the amber one, the children must remain in a sitting position.

Hold up the signals in random order for the children to carry out the corresponding action. The last child to respond to the signals each time sits out. The last child to be caught takes over the role of the traffic controller, holding up the cards to restart the game.

## Questions to ask
Have you ever watched the traffic lights changing colour? What does the red light mean? Have you noticed any other signs? What do you think it would be like if you could not see? What do you think it would be like if you could not hear?

## For younger children
Play the game using only red and green circles as stop and go signs.

## For older children
Introduce body awareness into the game with the green circle indicating to run quietly, the amber circle to sit up straight and the red circle to stand with feet together and arms by their sides.

**Follow-up activities**
• Take the children to a safe site to watch traffic lights changing colours.
• Invite children to cover their eyes and listen to a spoken command; challenge them to communicate to each other using gesture instead of words.
• Dance around to music played on a percussion instrument, when the music stops the children stop dancing and stand or sit still.
• Play instruments when the green card is held up, put them down for red, hold them still for amber.

# IN MY SACK

**Learning objective**
*To encourage sharing and taking turns while playing posting and delivering parcels.*

**Group size**
*Up to four children.*

## What you need
A post sack or similar, four large plastic tubs (post-boxes), red paint, a paint brush, four A4 pieces of card, scissors, four black marker pens, 20 small boxes, wrapping paper, Sellotape.

## Setting up
Paint the plastic tubs red to represent post-boxes. Make a sign for each box by writing on the card and taping it to the front of the post-box. Cover the small boxes in wrapping paper to represent parcels.

## What to do
Talk about how the post system works, asking if the children have ever received parcels through the post (perhaps on their birthdays or at Christmas).

Invite the children to go outdoors to play at posting parcels. Place the post-boxes all around the outdoor area. Share the presents between the children and ask them to post the parcels in the post-boxes.

Play at being the post worker, collecting the parcels up and then sharing them between the children for them to post again. Encourage the children to post the parcels in different post-boxes and make sure they all have a chance to deliver the parcels as well. As you play with the children, encourage them to share the parcels and take turns, working together if they prefer.

## Questions to ask
Have you ever posted a parcel? Have you ever received a parcel? Can you remember what was in your parcel? When do you get parcels? How do you feel when you are opening a parcel? Have you ever seen a post office van collecting and delivering parcels?

## For younger children
Use just one post-box and reduce the number of parcels.

## For older children
Make and wrap parcels. Help them to write name labels to stick onto the parcels. Set up a sorting office to sort the parcels before delivering them to each other.

**Follow-up activities**
• Play the game 'I sent a letter to my friend and on the way I dropped it'.
• Set up an outdoor post office.
• Let children write and post letters and invitations to each other.
• Visit a post office to buy some stamps.

# HANG IT UP

*Learning objective*
*To learn to look after belongings and to develop an understanding of personal hygiene.*

*Group size*
*Up to six children.*

## What you need
A set of clothes made up of a T-shirt, shorts/skirt/dress, vest, pants and socks for each child, a wash basket or plastic bowl each, a clothes horse.

## Setting up
Scatter the clothing separately all around the outdoor play area. Set up the clothes horse and place the plastic bowls nearby.

## What to do
Discuss personal hygiene with the children, explaining the reasons for changing our clothes regularly. Encourage the children to talk about their own experiences and routines at home. Ask them where they put their clothes when they take them off. Talk about washing dirty clothes, the machines we use and the soap and water used to get them clean again. Talk about the way the wind dries the washing hanging on the line.

Challenge the children to find a complete set of dirty clothes from the garments scattered all around the outdoor play space. Give each child a washing-up bowl to put the clothes in as they collect them and then ask them to hang them on the clothes horse.

To restart the game, the first child with a set of clothes hanging on the clothes horse is given the task of scattering the pretend washing all around the outdoor play area for another child to start again.

## Questions to ask
What happens when your clothes are dirty? What do you do to get them clean again? Where does all the dirty water go? How do you make yourself clean? How do you make your teeth clean?

## For younger children
Help younger children to find and hang up just two articles of clothing.

## For older children
Give the children pegs to hang up the clothes they collect.

**Follow-up activities**
• Wash dolls' clothes in a bowl of soapy water, rinse and hang them up to dry.
• Practise folding up sets of clothes to keep them neat and tidy.
• Place a large pile of clothes in a wash basket. Time how long it takes each child to hang them on a washing line.
• Visit a laundry to wash some clothes.

# SECRET PLACES

**Learning objective**
*To play co-operatively to create dens for imaginative role-play.*

**Group size**
*Up to six children.*

## What you needs
A 'secret', safe outdoor space, a table, a ground sheet, three or four old blankets, some string. CARE! Ensure that you can see the children at all times while they are playing, but let them think that their den is a secret one.

## Setting up
Make an outdoor den by covering a table with an old blanket. Encourage the children to use the den during outdoor play times.

## What to do
Explain to the children that they are going to make their own outdoor den in a hidden corner of your outdoor play space. Tell them that the den will be their secret place to play in. Help by tying the blankets onto a fence, draping them over a table or hanging them from trees according to what is available and the children's ideas. Challenge the children to design and build the dens of their dreams. Where possible find props to accompany their imaginary play, for example, use a picnic set and food to have a picnic inside the den.

Ask the children where they would like to build the den. Discuss the resources they will need. Talk about the reasons for building dens and find ways of making them safe, comfortable, secret, dark, light and so on.

## Questions to ask
Where do you want to build your den? What will you use to build it? How can you make your den a secret place? Have you ever had a den before? What is it like inside your den? What could you do inside the den? How many people can you fit in your den?

## For younger children
Help younger children to create their den and when it is finished, place domestic role-play props inside for them to pretend playing at home.

## For older children
Ask older children to think of a theme to go with their den and invite them to make their own props to use inside it.

**Follow-up activities**
• Invite some friends to a picnic inside the den.
• Set up a historical den with crafts and clothes from times past.
• Use the den as a 'quiet place' to look at books.

# DRESS UP WARM

*Learning objective*
*To begin independence by playing an outdoor dressing-up game.*

*Group size*
*Up to four children.*

## What you need

Four sets of outdoor winter clothes made up of a hat, a scarf and a coat, large enough to go on top of the clothes the children are already wearing.

## Setting up

Mark out a start and finishing line in a suitable outdoor play area. Space out the clothes between these points so that you have four hats in a row, four scarves in a row and four coats in a row.

## What to do

Ask the children to practise doing up and undoing the fasteners on their own outdoor clothing. Talk about the order in which they dress themselves in the morning and at bedtimes.

Take the children outdoors to the start line. Explain that each child has to run to the first row of clothes to put on a hat, to the second row of clothes to put on a scarf and to the third row of clothes to put on a top coat. When the children have put on all the clothing they must run to the finishing line. At the finishing line each child removes the outdoor clothes and folds them up neatly in a pile. Repeat the game several times to give the children plenty of practice to dress, undress and fold up the clothes.

## Questions to ask

Can you dress and undress yourself? What do you put on first? Can you do up the fasteners on your clothes? Can you put you own shoes on? What do you do with your clothes when you take them off?

## For younger children

Provide an adult helper to play the game with each child, helping them to put on the clothes and do up fasteners.

## For older children

Older children could play the game in the form of an obstacle race. Increase the amount of clothes they have to put on.

### Follow-up activities
- Sort piles of clothing into indoor/outdoor wear, summer/winter clothes or day/night clothes.
- Base the game upon a theme, dressing-up like clowns, scarecrows, pirates or knights.
- Make a display of clothes to wear in the rain, on the beach or to bed.
- Have a multicultural theme to the game, choosing several pieces of clothing from different countries (saris, large Mexican hats, kimonos and clogs).

# WINDY, WINDY WEATHER

**Learning objective**
*To learn to be co-operative and sensitive to the needs of others.*

**Group size**
*Up to four children.*

## What you need
A safe outdoor space on a windy day.

## What to do
Take the children outside on a windy day to experience the wind blowing. Invite the children to walk all around the outdoor area feeling the wind as it blows through their hair and into their faces. Explain to the children that you are going to play a game called 'Windy, windy weather'.

Gather the children into a huddle together to demonstrate how it is much warmer when you get close to each other. Now ask the children to hold hands in a long line, stand in the middle of the line yourself, holding the children's hands on either side. Walk together in a long line, face to the wind, chanting the words 'windy windy weather' several times. Then, unexpectedly call out 'windy windy weather we all come together' which is the cue to swing round into a huddle still holding hands. Walk on and after a few moments repeat the activity.

Ask the children how they can escape from the wind. Encourage them to try walking in different ways to avoid its force, include walking with their backs to the wind, with their faces down or with them partially covered with their hands. Can they find ways to protect one another from the wind by standing behind each other in a row? Find out what it is like to walk towards the wind or away from it.

## Questions to ask
What do you feel like on a windy day? Do you like the wind? Have you ever watched things blowing in the wind? How can you tell which way the wind is blowing? How can the wind help us?

### For younger children
Play the game with only two children at a time.

### For older children
Encourage older children to play in groups of three by themselves.

**Follow-up activities**
• Listen to the sound of the wind, and make up dances and chants to match the sounds you hear on a windy day.
• Chase leaves as they swirl round and round in corners of the outside play area.
• Watch the wind blowing in the trees.
• Make a simple kite to fly in the wind.

# DANCING DRAGONS

**Learning objective**
*To learn about other cultures by making dancing dragons to hang up outdoors in the wind.*

**Group size**
*Up to six children.*

## What you need
Photographs of Chinese dancing dragons used during celebrations, six sheets of white A4 paper, some brightly coloured felt-tipped pens, scissors, light-coloured cotton, Sellotape.

## Setting up
Photocopy the Chinese spiral dragon on page 62, one for each child.

## What to do
Show the children the pictures of dancing dragons and talk about when they are used in parades. Discuss Chinese celebrations and the way the dragon is used as a symbol. Give each child a photocopy of the Chinese spiral dragon and ask them to decorate the spiral shape like the brightly coloured dragons illustrated in the pictures. When the spirals are finished, cut along the dotted lines to make a spiral. Sellotape a piece of cotton to the tail end of the dragon, marked with the letter A.

Take the decorated dragons outside and hang them from trees or other suitable places. Wait for windy days and watch the dragons dancing in the wind.

## Questions to ask
What helps the spiral dragons to move? What is the dragon doing? Have you ever seen a picture of a dragon? What do dragons do? Do you think there are any real dragons? What would you do if you met one? Do you know any stories or songs about dragons?

## For younger children
Let younger children play outdoors with their dancing dragons, holding them as they flutter around in the wind.

## For older children
Encourage older children to add other decorations, such as streamers to their dragon. Encourage them to cut out their own spiral shapes to make dragons.

**Follow-up activities**
• Make a display of spirals hanging from the ceiling.
• Decorate the spirals to look like other creatures (snakes or fish).
• Work in small groups of three, pretending to be a dragon dancing. Make a mask for one child to wear, use a piece of silky cloth to cover the other two as they move around one behind the other.
• Sing 'Puff the Magic Dragon'.

*The outdoor activities in this chapter will encourage the development of children's understanding of their environment and of other people. Skills necessary for future work in history, geography, science and technology are introduced.*

# SQUASHED IN A SHOE

**Learning objective**
*To find out how people used to live by playing an outdoor game.*

**Group size**
*Ten to twelve children.*

## What you need
A large outdoor play space with a hard surface, a copy of the nursery rhyme 'There was an old woman who lived in a shoe', chalk.

## Setting up
Draw a large boot shape on the outdoor play surface with the chalk, just large enough for the group of children to stand inside.

## What to do
Read the rhyme 'There was an old woman who lived in a shoe' and discuss it with the children, encouraging them to learn the words. Explain some of the unusual vocabulary such as the word 'broth'. Tell them that a long time ago, families often lived in small homes with many more children in the family than today.

Invite the children to go outdoors to play the game. Explain that the boot shape chalked on the ground represents the old woman's home. Pretend you are the old woman and the children are outdoors playing. When the old woman calls out 'dinner time', the children must run and try to squash inside the home by standing close together, within the chalk outline of the boot. After a short while the old woman tires of having all the children squashed together inside the house making so much noise. To quieten them, she recites the rhyme. On hearing the words 'whipped them all soundly and sent them to bed', the children run back outdoors. The old woman chases them, trying to catch them.

## Questions to ask
How many children are there in your family? What did it feel like when you were squashed inside the boot? Where do you play at home? Why do you think the children were sent to bed without any broth?

## For younger children
Encourage the younger children to try to fit inside the boot and all recite the rhyme together.

## For older children
Older children could draw their own boot or shoe on the ground to play the game. Each child could take it in turns to be the old woman.

**Follow up activities**
• Put up a play tent for an outdoor home area.
• Display pictures of different types of homes.
• Make a vegetable broth to share outdoors on a cold day.
• Make a collection of old shoes and find matching pairs.
• Ask grandparents in to talk about their lives when they were children.

# BOTTLE BANKS

*Learning objective*
*To find out about*
*rainfall by collecting it*
*in gauges.*

*Group size*
*Up to six children.*

## What you need
For each child you need one 1 litre plastic bottle, scissors, 40cm length of string, a label, a permanent marker pen.

## Setting up
Place all materials outdoors on a flat surface.

## What to do
Begin by talking to children about the need to save rainwater. Give each child a plastic bottle and a marker pen. Explain that you are going to make a rain gauge to collect and measure the amount of rain that falls during the period of one week. (Choose a time when there is likely to be some rain.)

Help the children to make their own rain gauges. Make sure an adult cuts off the top of the plastic bottle. CARE! Cover sharp edges with masking tape. Invert it back into place to make a funnel through which the rain can collect and drip into the bottle. Use strong adhesive tape to attach the funnel to the bottle. Tape a length of string onto either side of the bottle to make a handle. Write each child's name on a sticky label and stick it to their bottle. Mark lines the width of thumb spaces from the bottom of the bottle to its neck.

masking tape covering cut edges

string

inverted bottle top.

Hang the bottles up outdoors, either from a tree or on a fence. Go outside daily for one week to check how much rain has collected in each bottle.

## Questions to ask
Where does the rain come from? How much rain will collect in the bottle during the week. How can the water be measured? How long will it take to fill the bottle up to the top? What can you do with the water? Are there any other ways you can save water?

## For younger children
Younger children will be fascinated to watch rainwater collecting in the bottles as it falls.

## For older children
Older children can work more independently to make their own rain gauges, writing their name labels to go on their bottles. Let them check the amount of rainfall at a set time each day and make records of their findings.

**Follow-up activities**
• Use the water collected in a safe, useful way, perhaps to water plants. CARE! Warn the children not to drink it.
• Compare the levels of rainfall collected in different sized bottles.
• Make a tally chart of how much rain falls in the week by making thumb prints on a piece of paper to correspond to the thumb measures marked on the bottles.

# PLAYFUL SHADOWS

*Learning objective*
To find out about the sun by exploring shadows.

*Group size*
Up to six children.

## What you need
A safe outdoor space on a sunny day, a piece of chalk for each child.

## Setting up
Tell the children how the sun creates shadows on a sunny day. Inform them that shadows outdoors are different lengths at different times of the day because of the way the sun moves across the sky. When the sun is high in the sky, shadows are short; when the sun is low, shadows are long. Show them that shadows touch them where they touch the ground (usually at their feet). Explain that shadows copy everything they do.

## What to do
Invite the children to go outside with you on a sunny day. Point out some of the shadows on the ground. Ask the children to make their own shadows by standing in a sunny spot. Ask them to stand in a space away from each other and tell them to stand still so that they can identify their own shadow. Encourage them to move around the outdoor space, watching their shadows as they follow them.

Challenge the children to find ways of making sure they can retain their whole shadow so that it is easily recognisable. Give them time to experiment. Encourage them to discover ways of moving so that the shadow seems to grow taller or smaller, or so that it disappears altogether. Take it in turns to play stepping on each others shadows.

## Questions to ask
When the sun goes in what will happen to your shadow? Can you make your shadow move? If you jump into the air, what happens to your shadow? Can you lose your shadow?

## For younger children
Look for shadows together; point out the way the children's shadow moves with them as they walk. Ask younger children if they can touch their shadows.

## For older children
Ask older children to make different shaped shadows by moving their bodies. Challenge them to make their shadows join them at different parts of their body other than their feet.

### Follow-up activities
• Play shadow games, chasing a friend around the outdoor play space. Shout 'stop', stand still and try to touch your friend's shadow with your foot.
• Make a sundial by standing a pencil on top of a cotton reel and gluing the cotton reel to a piece of white paper. Leave the sundial outdoors on a sunny day and mark where the shadow falls at hourly intervals.
• Show the children how to make animal shadows with their hands. Try to make a butterfly, a cat, a crocodile, a rabbit or a fox.

# A BOWLFUL OF BUBBLES

**Learning objective**
*To explore how bubbles are made and how they float in the air.*

**Group size**
*Up to four children.*

## What you need
Plastic sheeting or newspaper, aprons, a large bowl, a jug of water, a tablespoon, four tablespoons of washing-up liquid, twelve tablespoons of water, a few drops of glycerine, a drinking straw for each child.

## Setting up
Ensure all children wear aprons. Place some plastic sheeting or spread out newspaper on the ground before you start.

## What to do
Encourage the children to talk about the materials they are going to use, allow them to handle them carefully to encourage discussion. Explain that you are going to make a bubble mixture.

Help the children to measure out four tablespoonfuls of washing-up liquid and put this into the bowl. Help them to pour twelve tablespoons of water into the bowl and pour three or four drops of glycerine into the soapy mixture. Give the children a straw each. Encourage them to mix the liquids together with the straws and ask them to use the straws to blow bubbles. (CARE! Closely supervise the children and ensure that they do not try to drink the liquid.)

Encourage the children to continue blowing until they have made a bowlful of bubbles. Find ways of making the bubbles float in the air, perhaps by scooping up handfuls and flicking or shaking them off into the air.

## Questions to ask
How do the liquids feel? What happens to the mixture when they blow air into it? What happens to the bubbles when they flick them into the air? What happens when a bubble bursts? What happens when the bubble bumps into an object or touches the ground?

## For younger children
Give younger children their own pot of bubbles with a bubble blower and show them how to blow bubbles individually.

## For older children
Let older children experiment with the materials to make their own bubble liquid. Challenge them to cover the whole surface area being used with a mound of bubbles.

### Follow-up activities
• Buy some conventional bubbles and a range of bubble blowers to create different sized bubbles.
• Blow bubbles using you fingers to form a circle.
• Use sponges, whisks and brushes to make bubbles.
• Spray a deep layer of shaving foam into a bowl and encourage children to explore it, trying to make the foam float in the air by blowing it off their fingers.
• Try to make feathers or balloons float in the air by blowing them.

# GARDEN PATCH

*Learning objective*
To develop an
awareness of living
things and how to care
for them.

*Group size*
Up to six children.

## What you need
A patch of ground in the outdoor play space which can be dug up to create a small garden, pictures of gardens, small gardening tools, different types of plants, a watering can, some water.

## Setting up
Go outside and search for a small suitable plot of land, approximately one metre square, to create a small garden patch. Dig and prepare the soil ready for planting. If there is no suitable ground in the outdoor play space, put some soil in a deep tray or use a commercial growing bag for this activity.

## What to do
Discuss the pictures of the gardens with the children. Explain that they are going to create their own garden which could be a vegetable patch, a flower garden, a fragrant garden of perfumed flowers or a wild area to attract minibeasts.

Prepare the plants in advance, either by growing them from seed beforehand or by buying them ready grown. Choose fast-growing varieties, such as lettuce or radish to avoid disappointment. Give the children some small garden tools and ask them to make holes in the ground ready for the plants. Show them how to put the plants in, cover the roots with soil and water them.

Watch the plants as they grow and encourage the children to care for the garden patch throughout the year. Observe the changes throughout the seasons and watch the wildlife visiting or hiding in the patch.

## Questions to ask
What would you like to grow in the garden patch? What do you need to do to help the plants grow? What happens to the plants when they grow? What happens when the plants have finished growing? How do you grow? What do you need to help you grow?

## For younger children
Plant seeds in pots and encourage the children to water the plants and watch them grow.

## For older children
Let older children look after their own patch of garden independently.

**Follow-up activities**
• Grow tomato plants in a growing bag outside. Harvest the tomatoes and eat them when they are ready.
• Take children to visit different types of gardens.
• Visit a garden centre to buy seeds or plants.
• Create a miniature garden in a tray using foliage, leaves, stones and flowers found in the outdoor play area.

# BLOWING IN THE WIND

**Learning objective**
To develop an
understanding of how
the wind blows.

**Group size**
Up to four children.

pipe cleaner

holes   material

2nd pipe cleaner

pipe cleaner
threaded through
holes.

## What you need
A piece of light-weight material such as nylon or parachute material, pipe-cleaners, scissors, a conventional windsock or a picture of a windsock.

## Setting up
Take all the materials outdoors and place them on a ground sheet. Tie the example of a windsock in a suitable place to catch the wind, such as in a tree or on the fence.

## What to do
Go outside with the children and show them the windsock which you have or pictures of windsocks and discuss them and how they work. Explain that they are going to make their own windsocks.

Demonstrate step-by-step how to make the wind sock: cut a piece of material the same length as the pipe-cleaner and cut small holes one centimetre apart along the top edge. Thread the pipe cleaner through the holes and mould it into a ring shape, twist the end of the pipe-cleaner together. Using a second pipe-cleaner, fix the sock onto a place where it will catch the wind.

Observe what happens as the windsocks blow in the wind.

## Questions to ask
Which way is the wind blowing? What happens to the windsock when the wind changes direction? Look around you, what else can you see blowing in the wind? Have you ever seen a weather vane? What is it for?

## For younger children
Hang up a windsock outdoors and take the children outside to watch it blowing in the wind. Give the children a windmill to play with outdoors.

## For older children
Older children could work together in pairs or small groups to design and make their own wind socks, experimenting with a variety of materials to come up with the most efficient design.

**Follow-up activities**
• Use the photocopiable sheet on page 63 to make a wind flower: copy one for each child and let them decorate both sides of the template and the centre petals. Make up as directed.
• Go outdoors to watch the clouds blowing across the sky.
• Watch washing blowing on a washing line.

# NATURE SEARCH

*Learning objective*
To observe creatures living in the outdoor environment.

*Group size*
Up to six children.

## What you need
A safe outdoor area with some natural features such as plants, trees, bushes, branches or logs and stones. A large white sheet, plastic containers, magnifying glasses (one for each child).

## Setting up
Check the outside area to make sure there is nothing dangerous lying around. Before starting the search, inform the children of all safety issues, boundaries and ground rules.

## What to do
Go outdoors with the children, talking to them as you walk about safety issues and how we must care for all the little creatures in the outdoor environment.

Look on branches or logs, under large stones or on leaves for minibeasts. In particular look out for spiders in dark corners, woodlice along walls and near doors, slugs and snails behind flower pots, ladybirds, caterpillars, butterflies and moths among the leaves of trees and bushes.

Ask the children to describe the minibeasts they find and name them if they can. Encourage them to investigate the creatures by looking at them through the magnifying glasses.

Wherever possible observe the creatures without disturbing them. If necessary, shake a branch gently and allow the minibeasts to drop onto a small sheet or gather them gently into the small plastic containers. Remind the children that all living things must be treated with care and return them to their homes when the children have finished observing them.

## Questions to ask
What minibeasts live in the outdoors? Where will you look to find minibeasts? How many legs does a spider have? How many legs can you see on the minibeasts you found? Where might you find woodlice? When are you most likely to see slugs and snails?

## For younger children
Take younger children on a walk outdoors to look for minibeasts and talk about how we should care for them. Point out the creatures you see and name them for the children.

## For older children
Encourage older children to classify the minibeasts they find by comparing them with pictures in reference books. Let them record their observations by drawing the creatures they find.

**Follow-up activities**
• Make a wormery by collecting some worms and placing them in a plastic container with some damp compost. Place some leaves on top and put the container in a safe place for the children to watch.
• Collect and display books on minibeasts.
• Create a small pile of stones and leave it undisturbed for a few weeks to attract creatures.
• Count the number of butterflies you see outdoors on a summer's day.

# PEBBLE PARCELS

**Learning objective**
*To encourage
geographical enquiry
by following a route.*

**Group size**
*Up to six children.*

## What you need
A safe outdoor play space, ten medium-sized pebbles (golf ball-sized), ten pieces of brightly coloured material (large enough to wrap the pebbles inside), ten elastic bands, ten sheets of A5 paper and one large sheet of sugar paper, a pencil.

## Setting up
Wrap each pebble in a piece of the material and use an elastic band to secure the pebble inside. Place the ten markers on the ground outside to make a trail. CARE! Make sure the route you choose is safe and free from hazards. Choose places such as near the building, under a tree, in the shade, at the top or bottom of an incline, near the edge or in the middle of the play space, on a path or on the grass.

Mark each sheet of A5 paper at the top with a separate number from one to ten. Write 'start' on the first piece of paper.

## What to do
Invite the children to accompany you outdoors. Show them the first pebble parcel and demonstrate how you made it. Explain that you used ten parcels to make a trail. Invite them to follow it by looking for another pebble parcel. When the children find it, encourage them to look at the main features of their immediate surroundings and describe what they see. Jot down their descriptions on the piece of A5 paper marked with the number '2'. Continue following the trail until all ten pebble parcels have been discovered. Write down the main features of each place on the corresponding piece of A5 paper, in the order in which they were found. Make a map of the trail by displaying the descriptions on the sugar paper.

## Questions to ask
Where is this place? What is it like? What do you like about this place? What don't you like about it? What would it be like to live in this place? What can you see from this place? What kind of creature could live here?

### For younger children
Invite younger children to accompany you on the trail. Describe what you see as you go along. Give each child a pebble parcel to carry back with them. Invite them to make their own trails using the pebble parcels as markers.

### For older children
Extend the trail by using more pebble parcels. Make smaller parcels which are more difficult to spot. Encourage older children to make their own trails and maps for others to follow.

**Follow-up activities**
• Look at the real maps of the locality.
• Plot the trail on a simple map beforehand. Use the map to find the parcels.
• Cut around the outline of children's own painted footprints and cover them with transparent plastic 'tacky back'. Place the footprints in a long line on the ground to make a trail.
• Read the story of 'Hansel and Gretel'.

## CHAPTER FIVE

*Through these outdoor activities children will improve their gross and fine motor skills as they handle different tools, materials and equipment and take part in some action games. All the outdoor activities in this chapter will help develop vital physical skills.*

# HEFFALUMP

**Learning objective**
*To develop imagination and increase mobility by playing an action game.*

**Group size**
*Up to six children.*

## What you need
A copy of *Winnie the Pooh* A A Milne (Methuen), a safe outdoor play space, some white chalk.

## Setting up
Mark two chalk lines approximately 20m apart. Talk about the character Heffalump in the book *Winnie the Pooh*. Read the children the extract where Pooh is scared when he looks in the mirror and sees another Pooh, dreaming that there is a Heffalump under his bed.

## What to do
Explain that this is an enjoyable action game and choose one child to be the 'Heffalump' and to stand behind one of the chalk lines with his or her back to the others. Explain that Heffalump is dreaming about all the clever actions he can do and that he talks in his sleep, calling out an action such as 'hopping'. The children standing on the other chalk line must start to hop around. When Heffalump calls out another action such as 'jumping', the children must change actions from hopping to jumping.

Different actions are called out until Heffalump wakes up. He yawns loudly and all the children 'freeze'. Then Heffalump calls out, 'I'm hungry. I want a bun.' On the word 'bun' he chases the children thinking they have something for him to eat. The first child to be caught takes on the role of Heffalump.

## Questions to ask
Can you jump with two feet together? Can you hop on one leg? On the other leg? Can you skip? Can you run with little tiny steps? Can you walk with long strides? What do you think Heffalump would like to eat for his dinner? Do elephants really like buns? Can you imitate an elephant walk?

## For younger children
Play the game with an adult taking on the role of Heffalump. Limit the actions to only three choices such as walk, jump and run.

## For older children
Increase the difficulty of the actions, including bunny hops, jump high, walk with straight legs and walk keeping knees together.

**Follow-up activities**
•   Play other action games such as 'Tag', 'Off ground touch' and 'Bulldog'.
•   Create a dance around the elephant's dream, using all the actions he would like to be able to do.

# FOOTPRINTS ALL AROUND

*Learning objective*
To encourage increasing control and confidence by making and following footprints.

*Group size*
Up to six children.

## What you need
A safe outdoor pavement space, a mud patch, a jug of water, wellington boots or similar for each child, an outdoor brush.

## Setting up
Check out the outdoor area for safety. Find a patch of mud or create one by pouring water onto a patch of earth. Ask the children to put on their wellington boots.

## What to do
Go outside to the mud patch and talk to the children about the way animals leave trails of muddy footprints. Invite the children to step into the muddy patch one at a time and to make a trail of footprints. When they have all had a turn at leaving a trail, encourage the children to follow each other's trails by stepping carefully on top of each foot print already made.

Discuss the different footprints, comparing patterns and size. Ask the children to look at the patterns on the bottoms of each other's boots and challenge them to match the footprints to the right boots. Make long trails, straight trails, trails with many footprints, trails with spaced-out footprints and so on.

When the children have finished, pour some water onto the footprints and brush all the mud away leaving the pavement area clean. CARE! Ensure that the children wash their hands after touching the mud.

### Questions to ask
How can you tell which animal has left a trail? How many clear footprints can you make after standing in the muddy patch? How can you make different patterns with your footprints? How can you find out who or what made the footprints?

## For younger children
Take just two children out at a time to make muddy footprints. Make a muddy trail yourself for them to follow.

## For older children
Challenge older children to discover ways of disguising their footprints and encourage them to track each other around the outdoor play space, using any evidence they can.

### Follow-up activities
• Look for evidence of animal footprints around the outdoor play area. Use reference books to identify them.
• Make footprints with paint on a long roll of wallpaper placed outdoors on the ground. (CARE! Make sure the children do not slip and keep the paint on the paper.)
• Make plaster impressions by pouring wet plaster into footprints made in soft mud. When the plaster is dry, remove the footprint from it.

# FRUIT SHOP

*Learning objective*
*To develop physical control and awareness of space.*

*Group size*
*Up to eight children.*

## What you need
A large outdoor play space, some chalk, an apple, a banana and another piece of fruit (for example, a pear or star fruit).

## Setting up
Draw a circle, large enough to contain up to eight children in the middle of the outdoor play space.

## What to do
Give the children the opportunity to handle and talk about the fruit. Discuss the shapes, talking about the roundness of the apple, the long, curved banana shape and the odd-shaped pear.

Take the children to a suitable outdoor space, defining the boundaries and pointing out safety issues. Think up appropriate movements or shapes to represent each piece of fruit: an apple could be a small, tucked shape, a banana a long, stretched shape, a star fruit a wide body shape and a pear a bunny hop. Point out that the circle chalked in the middle of the space represents the fruit bowl. Explain that they are going to be moving around the space quickly and that they must listen to the commands which you will call out. Practise the actions used to represent the different fruits. To play the game, tell the children to run around the outdoor space as if on their way to the fruit shop to buy some fruit. Call out the name of a fruit (an apple) and the children must rush to the 'fruit bowl' and curl up in a ball as if they are an apple. The last child to respond is out and becomes the piece of fruit to be 'eaten' by the adult! Repeat using different fruit names and continue until all the fruit has been 'eaten'!

### Questions to ask
What kind of fruit do you like to eat? What shape does the fruit look like? Can you make a shape with your body that looks like a piece of fruit? Where do you buy fruit? Where do you put the fruit when you get home? Why do you eat fruit?

### For younger children
Reduce the number of commands, asking them to run to the fruit shop to buy just apples or bananas. Omit the fruit bowl and tell the children to make the shape you call out, on the spot.

### For older children
Increase the difficulty by having more actions to remember. Use five varieties of fruit as cues for action. Call out different fruits in quick succession to encourage the children to respond quickly.

**Follow-up activities**
• Cut the fruit into halves and quarters to share as refreshments after the game.
• Visit a fruit shop to buy some fruit.
• Slice the fruit and make prints with paint.
• Buy exotic fruit from different countries (pineapple, mango, passion fruit and kiwi) to extend knowledge and vocabulary.
• Use the fruit to feel, touch, smell, dissect and taste.

# CLEAR THE DECKS

**Learning objective**
*To develop manipulative skills and encourage an awareness of space and direction.*

**Group size**
*Up to six children.*

## What you need
A safe outdoor space, a large collection of small outdoor objects (quoits, balls, skittles, beanbags and spades) sufficient for each child to collect at least ten items.

## Setting up
Collect together the necessary equipment. Place the items at random all around the outdoor play space.

## What to do
Take the children outdoors and discuss the boundaries and safety issues before the game starts by reminding the children where they can go and what they can do.

Point out all the items scattered around the ground and explain that the children are going to try to collect them all together to clear the decks. The child who manages to collect the most items has a turn at scattering them all around the outdoor play area in order for the game to start again.

Invite each child to choose a base where they can safely store their items until they count them up at the end of the game. Ensure all the children are aware of each other's home base so that there is no confusion about which items they pick up.

Play the game several times.

## Questions to ask
How can you clear up the toys scattered all around the outdoor play space? How can you collect lots of items in one go? Where are you going to put the toys to count them? How many toys have you collected?

## For younger children
Scatter fewer toys around a smaller space for younger children to collect. Give them a container to carry them back to the counting spot.

## For older children
Increase the number of items to be collected and hide them around the outdoor play area to increase the difficulty of the game. Encourage older children to work in pairs or small groups.

**Follow-up activities**
• Sort the items collected.
• Play the game using small items such as marbles.
• Use playing cards for the children to collect up. Score five points for an ace, four points for a king, three points for a queen and so on. Encourage the children to count up their individual scores.

# FOLLOW ME

*Learning objective*
*To develop physical control and co-ordination by following a leader.*

*Group size*
*Up to six children.*

## What you need
A safe outdoor area suitable for an action game, an adult helper.

## Setting up
Check the outdoor play area for safety. Remind children of the safety issues and boundaries involved in playing an action game outdoors.

## What to do
Take the children outdoors and explain that you are going to play a game. Ask the adult helper to keep an eye on the children, as you will have your back to them throughout the game!

Tell the children that you will be leading the game and that they should copy every move you make. Position them so that you have your back to them. Move around the outdoor play space, encouraging the children to follow, copying the actions which you make. Vary the type of movement by running, skipping, hopping, jumping and walking in random order for several minutes.

## Questions to ask
Can you copy every move your friend makes? Can you follow the leader? Do you ever copy anyone else? What is it like when someone copies you?

## For younger children
Choose simple actions to suit the children's abilities. Position an adult to face the children as they are following the leader to give them encouragement.

## For older children
Increase the difficulty of the actions and change from one movement to another in quick succession. Let them take turns to be the leader.

**Follow-up activities**
• In pairs, copy each other's movements. Pretend to be looking in a mirror, matching each other's movements face on.
• Copy facial expressions.
• Repeat some tongue-twisters.
• Play secret whispers, passing on a whispered phrase around a small group. The last child repeats the phrase out loud to see if it is still the same as when the whispers began.
• Play the game 'Simon Says'.

# BUILD IT!

*Learning objective*
*To use a variety of*
*construction materials*
*outdoors.*

*Group size*
*Up to six children.*

## What you need
A variety of building materials such as small wooden/plastic blocks, small wooden planks, baker's trays, milk crates, short pieces of plastic guttering or pipes. A selection of props to use with these construction materials such as cars, play people, animals or dinosaurs.

## Setting up
Take the materials outdoors to a suitable space and set them up to make towers, bridges and slopes according to the pieces of equipment you have available. Place the props invitingly around the constructions which you have set up.

## What to do
Take the children outdoors to the construction set-up and explain that they can use the materials available to set up their own scenes to play with the toys. Demonstrate how to build a few simple constructions to give the children ideas on how to get started. You could place a plank across two milk crates to make a bridge to drive the cars across for example, or you could make a ragged tower to represent a dinosaur's habitat, or rest a piece of plastic guttering to make a slope to roll cars down and so on.

Encourage the children to move the materials around the outdoor play space and to set up their own construction scenes, taking care not to bump into anyone else as they move.

## Questions to ask
What can you build with these materials? Can you make some slopes to roll the cars down? Can you make some high towers for the play people to climb? What can you make with the planks of wood? What do you need to make a bridge? Have you ever seen a house being built?

## For younger children
Limit the range of building materials you set out. The main focus for younger children will be the process of carrying the objects around the garden or piling them up on top of each other.

## For older children
Give older children the opportunity to make more permanent constructions that can be left outdoors and used for a few days. Encourage older children to work co-operatively on joint ventures.

### Follow-up activities
• Take the children to a safe site to watch some building in process.
• Give the children some small household bricks, sand and water to 'build' with.
• Make a visit to see, or walk over, a bridge.
• Visit a builder's merchants to buy small pieces of building materials to use for building in the outdoor play space.

# THROUGH THE TUNNEL

**Learning objective**
*To develop an awareness of space and other people.*

**Group size**
*Up to ten children.*

## What you need
A safe outdoor play space.

## Setting up
Check the outdoor area and prepare it for use by removing any dangerous items which might cause the children to trip or injure themselves.

## What to do
Take the children outdoors and define the area and remind children of any safety or ground rules. Explain the game they are to play is an

action game, whereby the leader chases them around the outdoor play space to try and touch them. When they are touched, they have to stand with their legs apart to make a tunnel through which one of the other children will crawl to release them from captivity.

Explain that they have three 'lives' and when they are caught for the third time they are out of the game. The last child to be touched takes over the role of leader for the next game. If all the children are caught out and there is no one left to crawl through the tunnels, the leader can opt to start the game again or nominate a new leader.

Play the game with you as the leader to start with. Play until each child who wishes to have a turn as the leader, has done so.

## Questions to ask
Can you make a tunnel with your legs? Have you ever been through a tunnel? What is it like going through a tunnel? Where do you see tunnels? What animals make tunnels in the ground?

## For younger children
Decrease the number of chances so that younger children are out on the first touch. They could make the tunnel shape with their legs to indicate when they are out.

## For older children
Older children could play with two leaders to increase the level of difficulty for the children being chased. They could make the tunnels by using their arms as well as their legs instead of making them with just their legs.

**Follow-up activities**
• Take the children to visit a dark tunnel.
• Go on a train ride through a tunnel.
• Make a long people tunnel by asking the children to stand with their legs apart or on their hands and knees next to each other. Take it in turns to crawl through the tunnel.
• Try to dig a small tunnel in an outdoor sandpit.

# COLLECTING TAILS

**Learning objective**
*To move confidently with increasing control.*

**Group size**
*Up to ten children.*

## What you need
A safe outdoor play space, appropriate dress for outdoor physical activity, some coloured strips of parachute material, approximately 5cm wide by 50cm long.

## Setting up
Check out the outdoor area for safety, removing any dangerous objects.

## What to do

Take the children outdoors, reminding them of any safety rules, and set the boundaries for the game. Explain to the children that they are going to pretend to be animals running away from a hunter who is trying to catch their tails.

Give them each a strip of parachute material and tell them to tuck it down the back of their shorts or into their waistband so that it hangs down the back like a tail. Chase the children around the outdoor play area, trying to catch hold of the 'tails'. The game is over when all the 'tails' have been retrieved.

Talk to the children about taking care not to bump into one another by looking where they are going. Encourage them to use all the space and remind them not to hold on to their 'tails' or tuck them too far down their shorts.

## Questions to ask
What animals have long tails? Have you ever seen any animals with long tails? Where have you seen animals with long tails? What happens to the tails when the animal runs? What happens to the tail when the animal is sad or happy?

## For younger children
Play the game at a slower pace by asking younger children to walk around like animals. Have smaller groups of three or four children playing at a time. Demonstrate how gentle you have to be when you take the tail.

## For older children
Older children will enjoy taking it in turns to be the hunter as well as the animals. Have a time limit to see who can collect the most tails during the time set.

**Follow-up activities**
• Play cat-and-mouse chase games around the outdoor play area.
• Look at pictures of animals with tails in reference books.
• Visit a zoo or farm to look at animals with tails.
• Talk about the use animals have for their tails, how some monkeys have prehensile tails, how cows flick flies off their backs with their tail and so on.

*Outdoor play can provide many situations to encourage creative development and for children to use their imaginations. These activities help children to express their ideas and feelings.*

# MAGIC SHOES

**Learning objective**
To encourage physical control and body awareness.

**Group size**
Up to six children.

## What you need
A safe outdoor play space.

## What to do
Ask the children to imagine that they have magic shoes which make them dance. Explain that you will call out an action and they must respond by changing their actions to suit. So you may call out: 'put on your walking shoes/your hopping shoes/your skipping shoes/your running shoes'.

Invite the children to dance around the outdoor play area pretending to wear magic shoes and whenever you call out a different action they must change their movements. Encourage the children to travel in different directions as they dance. Remind them to take care not to bump into each other.

## Questions to ask
How can you dance when you wear magic shoes? What other types of shoes do people wear? Do you like new shoes? What are your favourite shoes? Why do you like them? What kinds of shoes do people wear in winter? What do they wear in summer? Do you have any special shoes?

## For younger children
Pretend to be wearing magic shoes yourself and dance around the outdoor play area. Ask younger children to copy the way you dance. Invite them to make up their own dance steps for each other to copy.

## For older children
Extend the ways the magic shoes make the children dance to include more difficult movements such as jumping, twisting, tiptoeing, sliding, bouncing, springing and prancing.

Encourage the children to make contrasting movements, sometimes dancing fast, sometimes dancing slow, sometimes dancing with little light steps, other times with big heavy ones.

**Follow up activities**
• Collect old shoes to set up a shoe shop outdoors.
• Make a collection of shoes to display.
• Put shoes into pairs, count and order them in size.
• Tell the story *Puss in Boots*.

# GROW A SCARECROW

**Learning objective**
To explore three-dimensional shape and form using discarded flowerpots.

**Group size**
Up to four children.

## What you need
Picture of a scarecrow, eight 3inch/7.6cm reclaimed flowerpots, two 5inch/12.7cm reclaimed flowerpots, ball of string, ten or more cotton reels, some strips of brightly coloured parachute material or cotton approximately 2cm wide by 30cm long, a marker pen, a pair of scissors, a blanket or ground sheet, a small patch of garden.

## Setting up
Wash the flowerpots if necessary. Spread the blanket or ground sheet out in a suitable outdoor working area. Place all the resources on the ground sheet.

material strips tied to make hands and feet.

## What to do
Explain to the children the concept of a scarecrow, showing them a picture as a guide.

Ask the children to help you join the flowerpots together to make two arms and two legs. Separate the flowerpots by threading a cotton reel between them and knotting a piece of parachute material to keep the pots apart. Tie the arms and legs onto one of the large flowerpots to make a body, in the same way as you joined the smaller pots to make arms and legs, using a cotton reel and some parachute material tied between the pots to separate them.
Fix the head onto the rest of the body.

Tie the parachute material all over the string at the top to look like hair and draw a face on the head flowerpot. Hang the finished model on a fence or in a tree.

knotted parachute material or other.

parachute material

cotton reel

## Questions to ask
Have you ever seen a scarecrow or a picture of one before? Why do farmers put scarecrows in their fields? What happens to a scarecrow when it is windy? How else could you stop the birds eating seeds and plants?

## For younger children
Make individual scarecrows using one flowerpot, drawing a face on one side and tying five or six pieces of parachute material through the drainage holes in the bottom of the pot. Place on the top of empty plastic lemonade bottles standing up in the garden patch.

## For older children
Encourage older children to work co-operatively in small groups to create their own scarecrows from the materials.

**Follow-up activities**
• Learn and sing the song 'Dingle, Dangle Scarecrow'.
• Make up a scarecrow dance using the flowerpot scarecrows.
• Thread beads and cotton reels together to make other shapes.
• Use up-turned flowerpots to make some stilts by tying long lengths of string onto either side of the pots. Try to balance and walk on them.

# SANDY GIRL/BOY

*Learning objective*
*To encourage children to express their feelings through movement and dance.*

*Group size*
*Up to eight children.*

## What you need
A large, safe outdoor play space. A copy of the song 'There's a little sandy girl', from *This Little Puffin* (Puffin).

## Setting up
Check the outdoor area to ensure there are no hazards for the children playing.

## What to do
Take the children outdoors and ask them to form a circle by holding hands together. Choose a child to be the sandy girl or boy (the traditional name for the child in this action song).

The sandy girl/boy is sitting on a stone weeping because there is no one to play with. Explain that they are going to play this circle game where they sing the words.

The children repeat the verse, singing the sounds *'la la la la la la la la'* and clapping their hands as the sandy girl/boy jumps up to choose a child to dance in the ring with her/him. That child then becomes the sandy girl/boy sitting in the middle of the ring as the children dance around again. Repeat the activity until all the children have been chosen to dance in the ring with the sandy girl/boy.

## Questions to ask
Why do you think the sandy girl or boy is weeping? What could you do to cheer her/him up? Why do you sometimes cry? How do you feel when you cry? What cheers you up when you are sad? What makes you happy?

## For younger children
Learn the song and take it in turns to dance around the outdoor play space as the other children sing and clap.

## For older children
Encourage older children to think of a different dance each time they join Sandy in the middle of the ring.

## Follow-up activities
• Play other ring games such as 'The farmer's in his den', 'There was a princess long ago', 'Ring-o-ring-o-roses', 'Here we go round the mulberry bush'.
• Make up actions and dances to other favourite rhymes.
• Discuss feelings and talk about the importance of being kind and playing with each other.

# OUTDOOR BANDS

*Learning objective*
*To explore sound and*
*respond imaginatively*
*by setting up music*
*bands.*

*Group size*
*Up to six children.*

### What you need
A frame or similar to hang up pots and pans, several metal pots, pans, jugs and serving spoons (at least two or three for each child), some string.

### Setting up
Check out the availability of a sturdy outdoor frame on which to hang the kitchen implements to make the bandstand. If there is nothing suitable, improvise by using a clothes horse fixed securely to a fence, tree or wall, or by making up a frame with some large outdoor construction materials such as Quadro. Take the resources outdoors and place them on the ground near the frame.

### What to do
Go outdoors with the group and invite them to handle and explore how to make sounds with the kitchen implements. When they are ready explain that the implements are going to be tied onto the frame to make a set of band instruments which they can use outdoors.

Tie the pots and pans to the frame by threading the string through the handles of the implements. Let them dangle down from the frame on the string so that they will bang together in the wind even when the children are not playing with them.

Challenge the children to make noises by banging the pots and pans with serving spoons also tied onto the frame as before. Encourage the children to respond through dance and movement to the sounds they make and hear.

### Questions to ask
What will happen when the pots and pans knock together in the wind? What instruments do you know or have you seen? Can you make loud noises with the outdoor band?

### For younger children
Give younger children their own pots, pans and spoons to play with outdoors. Encourage them to bang them together to make sounds.

### For older children
Encourage older children to create simple tunes or repeated patterns of sound and movement for others to watch or copy.

**Follow-up activities**
• Invite musicians to show children how they play real instruments.
• Set up a display of percussion instruments for children to experiment with.
• Hang wooden objects from the frame and give the children wooden spoons to create different outdoor sounds.
• Sit down in a quiet, safe spot to listen to the sounds going on all around the outdoor play space.

# SPINNING SPLODGES

*Learning objective*
To make a simple
spinner.

*Group size*
Up to six children.

## What you need
Scissors, a variety of types of papers, tissues, thin
card, writing materials, paint, brushes, paper-
clips, sycamore seeds, photocopiable page 64.

## Setting up
Collect sycamore seeds with the children when
they are in season and store them ready to use.
Talk about the way some seeds are transported
around in the air by the wind until they
drop to the ground and find a growing
place. Copy photocopiable page 64,
one for each child.

## What to do
Using the photocopiable sheet, encourage the
children to cut around the lines as indicated in
the diagram. Offer help where necessary. Show
them how to fold the paper along the dotted lines
and fix the bottom together with a paper-clip,
which will act as a weight to keep the spinners
upright as they spin from a height to the ground.
Paint brightly coloured splodges of paint
according to the diagram.

Take the spinners outdoors and drop
from a height if possible, perhaps by
standing on a low wall. Make up
different sized spinners using different
types of paper and add more/fewer
paper-clips to the base of the spinners.
Compare what happens when the
different spinners are dropped from a
height.

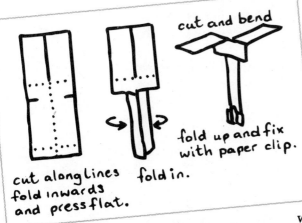

cut and bend

fold up and fix
with paper clip.

cut along lines
fold inwards
and press flat.

fold in.

## Questions to ask
Why do sycamore seeds need to fly?
What happens to the paint splodges
when the spinners are dropped to the floor?
Can you spin around on the spot? How do you feel when you spin?

## For younger children
Make up the spinning splodges for the children and let them watch
as you drop them from a height.

## For older children
Ask older children to design their own spinners using a variety of
materials.

**Follow-up activities**
• Add curled or
straight feathers to
the wings of the
spinners; compare
what happens.
• Make a display of
spinning toys.
• Play a game with
a spinning Jenny.
• Take the children
to see a spinning
wheel in a museum
or craft fair.
• Spin hoola hoops
on the floor and keep
them going.

# ICE ART

*Learning objective*
To create three-dimensional pictures by freezing leaves in ice.

*Group size*
Individually or in pairs.

## What you need
A safe outdoor play space with access to fallen leaves, a small recycled polystyrene or plastic food tray, a jug of water. Carry out this activity during freezing weather.

## Setting up
Prepare an example in advance. Place three small brightly coloured leaves in a tray. Pour water into the tray so that the leaves are fully submerged or until the water in the tray is approximately 2cm deep. Place outdoors in a safe place to freeze overnight.

## What to do
Go outside with the children and show them the tray of frozen leaves you prepared in advance. Take the ice out of the tray and let the children handle the frozen ice as you explain how you made it. CARE! Make sure that children do not lick the ice or put it into their mouths. Hold up the ice block to the light, pointing out the leaves you have frozen inside it.

Invite the children to go off to collect some leaves to use to make their own ice picture. Ask them to arrange the leaves in the small food tray and pour some water on top of the leaves as before. Leave outdoors overnight if weather permits or place in a freezer if necessary until the next day.

When the water has frozen, remove from the tray and take the pictures back outdoors. Encourage the children to handle the icy pictures and look at them as they glisten in the light. Place the pictures in a safe outdoor spot to watch them slowly melt away.

## Questions to ask
What will happen to the leaves when the ice melts? What patterns have you seen outdoors when it is frosty? What else can you do with ice?

## For younger children
Help younger children to freeze just one leaf in water.

## For older children
Older children could make more complex ice art by freezing an arrangement of several leaves in a tray.

**Follow-up activities**
• Make ice balloons by filling a balloon with water and freezing it. When frozen, peel off the balloon to reveal the beautifully smooth sphere of ice. Invite children to handle it and talk about its properties.
• Use fruit peel to make funny frozen faces using the same method.
• Freeze arrangements of other small objects to make ice art.

# VEGETABLE PEOPLE

**Learning objective**
*To create characters using vegetables for imaginary play.*

**Group size**
*Individually, in pairs or small groups.*

## What you need
A collection of odd-shaped root vegetables (carrots, potatoes, parsnips, swedes, turnips), pipe-cleaners, scooping tools, cocktail sticks, permanent marker pens, plastic sheeting or newspaper.

## Setting up
Make up some examples of vegetable people in advance and place them outdoors in a suitable place, such as along the top of a low wall or on an outdoor table. Take all the materials outdoors and place them on a piece of plastic sheeting on the ground. If no plastic sheeting is available, spread newspaper on the ground.

## What to do
Invite the children to look at the characters you made in advance and invite them to describe the characters and name the vegetables you used to make them. Ask the children questions to find out what they know about vegetables.

Allow each child to choose some vegetables to make their own characters. Demonstrate to them how to scoop out the centre of large vegetables, how to make eye holes, ears and a mouth. Help the children to join some of the vegetables together using the lolly sticks or pipe-cleaners. CARE! Make sure that the children do not hurt themselves or others with the sticks, or that they do not put vegetables in their mouth to eat. Ensure that all sharp ends are safely stuck into the vegetables. Show them how to draw a funny face on the head to personalise their characters. Encourage them to involve the characters in their imaginative play. Group them together as if they are a vegetable family living in the outdoor play space.

## Questions to ask
How do things grow? How do you grow? What vegetables have you used to make your character? Is your vegetable person mean, scary, friendly, ugly? What do you think will happen to your vegetable person if you leave it in the outdoor play area?

## For younger children
Younger children will enjoy choosing funny-shaped vegetables for an adult to draw a face on.

## For older children
Older children can work independently to create their own vegetable characters, drawing a design before they start to make them.

**Follow-up activities**
• Use the vegetables to make vegetable prints.
• Make characters from other food such as fruit, bread or pasta.
• Use the characters to make an outdoor display.
• Take the children to choose and buy their own vegetables from a grocer's shop.

# A WAXY RUB

***Learning objective***
*To explore the texture and pattern of outdoor objects.*

***Group size***
*Individuals, pairs or groups of four.*

## What you need
Several sheets of thin white drawing paper, chubby wax crayons in dark colours (one for each child), a safe outdoor space with a variety of objects such as bricks, drainage covers, pavement slabs, tree trunks. CARE! Ensure children do not put their fingers in exposed holes.

## Setting up
Check out the outdoor area for safety and remove any dangerous objects. Locate objects suitable for a wax rubbing.

## What to do

Take the children outdoors and give them each a wax crayon and a sheet of white drawing paper. Invite them to go on a walk looking for objects with different patterns and textures. Spend a little time pointing out the different shapes, textures, colours, materials and patterns. Explain that the children are going to make a rubbing to record some of the things they have seen outside.

Demonstrate how to make a rubbing by placing the paper on top of the chosen object. Holding the paper in one hand and using the wax crayon with the other hand, rub the wax crayon over and over the surface of the paper. Encourage the children to make several prints of the same object, using different colours and rubbing the wax crayon in different ways. Compare and contrast the finished results with each other and with the object used to make the rubbing.

## Questions to ask
Ask the children to explain what they are doing. What is the easiest way to use the crayon to make a wax rubbing? Where could you find a pattern made up of lines? What else is made of wax?

## For younger children
Take younger children out individually to make their wax rubbings. Show them exactly what to do, emphasising that they should only rub the crayon over the paper not the object itself!

## For older children
Let older children work co-operatively in pairs to make large wax rubbing and select their own objects to do rubbings from. Give them specific tasks, such as making a rubbing of a tree or a pavement slab or finding a pattern made with curves or straight lines.

**Follow-up activities**
• Visit a site to make brass rubbings.
• Make leaf rubbings.
• Find other ways of recording the patterns and textures found in the outdoor environment.
• Look out for other types of prints in reference books.

# PHOTOCOPIABLES

**Name** _____

| | Monday | Tuesday | Wednesday | Thursday | Friday |
|---|---|---|---|---|---|
| cloudy | | | | | |
| sunny | | | | | |
| rainy | | | | | |
| windy | | | | | |
| frosty | | | | | |
| snowy | | | | | |

**Name** _____

Cut along the black lines. Decorate the birds and
attach them with cotton to two straws.

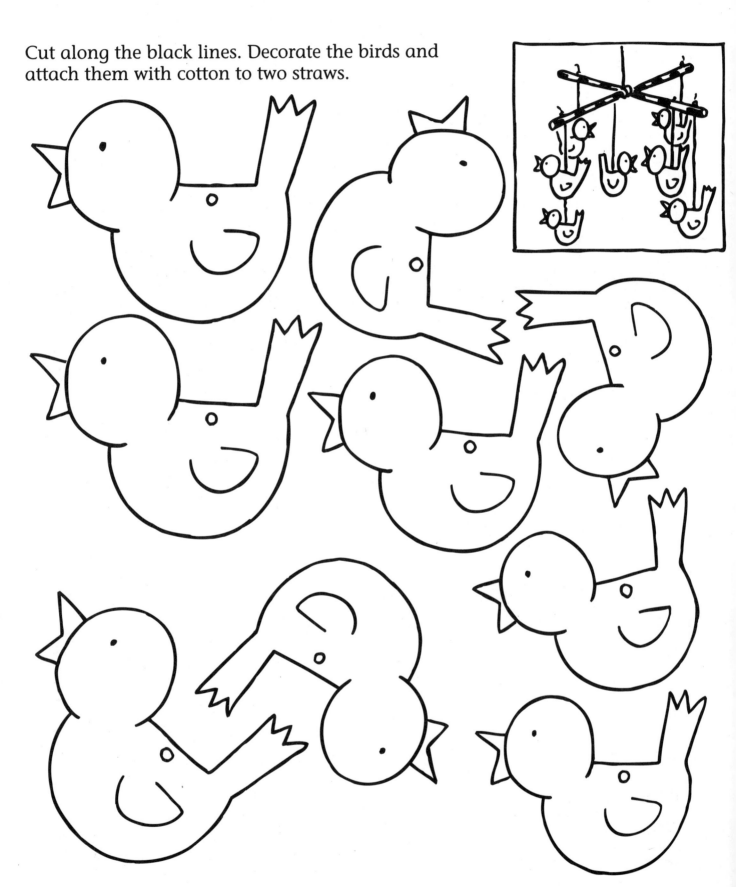

**Name** _____

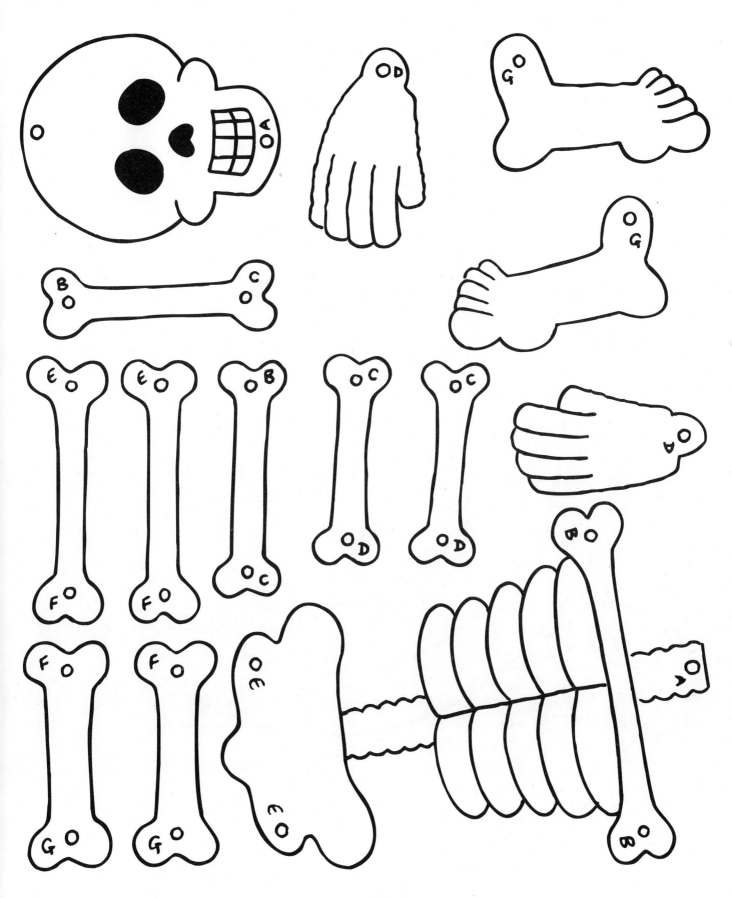

**Name** _____

Decorate and cut along
the black lines to make
a spiral dragon.

Name _____

Cut along the bold outlines, fold along the dotted ones. Fold
corners marked A into the centre spot. Make a small hole through
the centre and through the middle of each corner piece. Cut out
the petals below and arrange them in the centre of your flower.
Attach the parts to a straw using a butterfly clip.

**Name** _____

Make two
spinners by
cutting along
the solid black
lines and
folding along
the dotted ones.

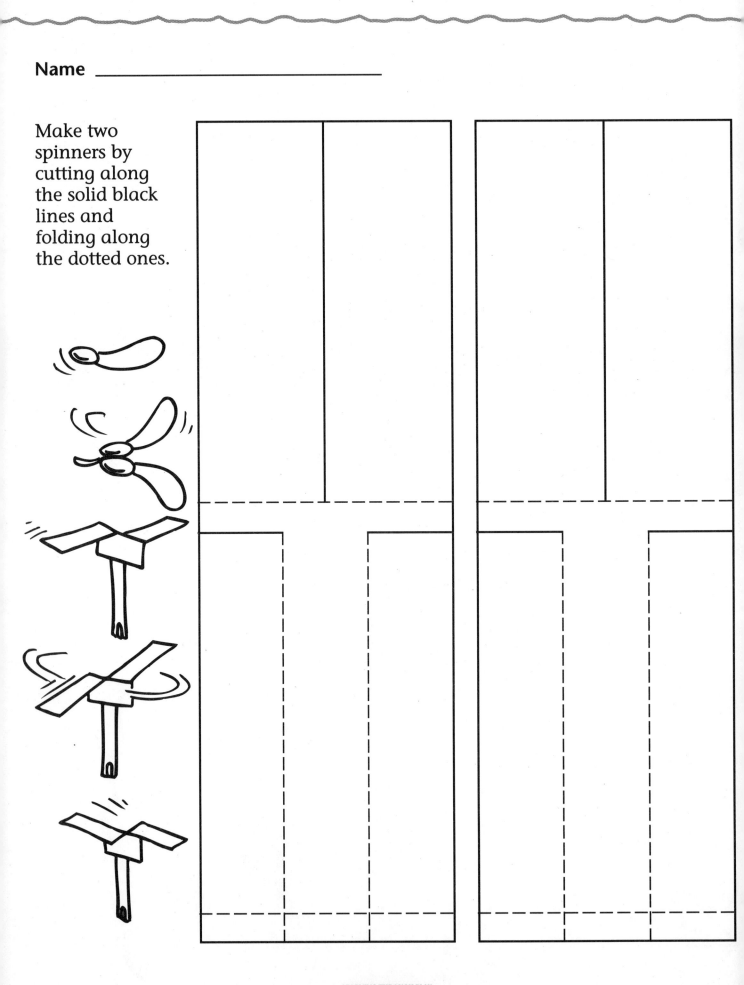